In Touch With the Miraculous
FRAGMENTS OF AN ENDURING TEACHING

Rolando Altamirano

Blue Logic Publications

© 2010

A Blue Logic Publication
P.O. Box 772
Oregon House, CA 95962
www.bluelogic.us

All rights reserved © 2010
by
Rolando Altamirano
Copyright throughout the world

No part of this book may be reproduced or transmitted in any form or by any means, graphic, electronic, or mechanical, including photocopying, recording, taping, or by an information storage retrieval system, without permission in writing from the publisher.

ISBN 978-1-607-25001-2

Printed in the United States of America

Some there be that by due steps aspire to lay their just hands on that golden key that opes the palace of eternity, to such my errand is.

John Milton

Foreword

A teaching of this nature can only be presented in fragments. Its scale is so vast and it involves the work of so many people, throughout so many years, that to aim at producing a single document to describe the whole would prove preposterous. Moreover, this teaching is alive now and it continues to change its form and become more precise and refined. If one wished to pin it down, the endeavor would be like to try to write the biography of someone who not only is not what he was, but he is not what he will be, and will almost certainly outlive one.

However, our School has produced and continues to produce, in an organized way, many texts that describe how this teaching has developed throughout the years. (The first publication proves how it all started practically at the level of a magnetic center). Should a study of the whole be pursued, these texts could very well be the thin red line.[1]

One must also bear in mind that the teaching is presented by an individual, and it illustrates mainly the way this individual was led to it, absorbed it and put it into practice.

---

[1] Some of them are "Via del Sol", "Mount Carmel Journal", "Renaissance Journal", "Fellowship Forum", "The Apollonian", Creating a Soul,, Self Remembering, and "Thoughts from the Teacher".

In Touch With The Miraculous

As the title of this document suggests, this teaching is based mainly on the work of Gurdjieff and Ouspensky, but also of other teachers that have followed them as well. This is an ancient teaching designed for modern man. It is also very simple, intended for simple, ordinary people.

Despite the fact that these fragments are small and scattered (as they are not written chronologically), they do convey the nature of the vessel they mean to portray. Yet understanding of an esoteric teaching can only be gained through direct experience and personal work. In order to grasp the teaching one must BE the teaching.

Understandably, some of the names have been omitted or modified for privacy purposes. Also, whenever a conversation or an event is referred to, the dialogues and circumstances are based on my memory alone. Someone else present at the same event might have a different angle on the subject, thus providing a touch of relativity.

Dear reader, I hope you find this useful.

With Love,

Rolando Altamirano
Apollo, October 2009

A few familiar facts and agents bring home unmistakably to our consciousness the existence of powers that work all around us, however, these may oftentimes elude our senses... they bear witness to that Great First Cause Who ordained them and Who rules them.
                                    Cristina Rossetti.

Introduction

Once upon a time in one's life one remembers that above and beyond human beings there exist invisible beings of a higher nature, or Higher Forces, whose task is to cultivate a number of individuals for a specific purpose, just as people cultivate a number of plants for specific purposes. Eventually one begins to recognize how they arrange everything that happens through one and around one: from the way one is born, to one's relations, and to the events that shape one's psychological makeup. One also sees that almost nothing in one's life is accidental, and points to a reality within one as invisible as Higher Forces themselves.

He who participates in the expansion of consciousness sooner or later recognizes the work of Higher Forces behind it. For just as the spark of consciousness is inherent in us, so is our ability to become aware of conscious beings no longer bound to a physical body.

What George Gurdjieff called the "magnetic center" is born within the physical body from the impulse to remember what is forgotten at the moment of conception. The growth of the magnetic center depends on one's efforts to attract the right influences that help it develop. Influences can come from a song, from a poem, from a religious text, from a work of art, etc. They may also come in the form of shocks provided by fate or by Higher Forces themselves. These shocks remind one that "something" within one exists for all eternity, and that the moment it is cast in the physical body it falls into oblivion. One also understands that the overwhelming mechanical laws that govern the physical body act as an almost invincible opponent to its reawakening. This "something" we call the divinity within.

Throughout the years we have verified that a magnetic center does not develop from the physical body itself, for the physical body is exclusively interested in its comfort and maintenance. A magnetic center developed from the physical body may also relate to the idea that there exist Higher Forces monitoring life on earth, but it perceives them as mere fatherly figures that have given one life and should provide everything necessary for one's organic existence. According to this view, all one needs to do is keep a certain profile and Higher Forces will take care of the rest. The shape of this profile is given by the creed one did choose or was given by chance. In this case one's relationship to Higher Forces is based on the necessity to safeguard and enhance one's organic existence, and eventually secure a better reality once this one comes to its inevitable end.

It has been revealed that consciousness varies by degree of wakefulness at a given moment, and we have also discovered that as a whole it has levels of development.

One can verify its level of development in one's ability to recognize the work of Higher Forces as well as the intensity of one's drive and will to assist them in their efforts towards its awakening: Some people's efforts are generally feeble and sporadic, while others' are focused and steady from the beginning.

In order to give the Fourth Way a right valuation a man must have thought and felt and been disappointed in many things beforehand.

Gurdjieff

I

As I perceived the work of Higher Forces, I was certain that there must be a way to establish a relationship with them just like Jesus, Socrates, Quetzalcoatl, Mohammed and others had done and ultimately became like them. I was also sure that somewhere in the world there had to be people working anonymously with Higher Forces, just like these spiritual leaders worked anonymously during their lifetime. Only much later their work became popular and, in some sad cases, it eventually became a religion. I knew I had to find someone just like one of these people. I tried to find one within the religion through which I was raised. So my first move in that direction was to ask to be sent to a Christian monastery, sure to find them there. I was twelve years old.

Most individuals in the monastery produced fear in me, to the extent that I could not imagine speaking with confidence about my understanding of Higher Forces. Their indisputable view of Higher Forces was in the church-appointed saints and angels who acted as mediators between men and God. I was ready to work with this view. Its dubious part, however, was that the leaders of the monastery acted as mediators between angels and us sinners. There were strict rules in the monastery, a tight hierarchy, and cruel means to keep everything in order (Christianity was imparted in Mexico by cruel and atrocious methods in the XVI century). In general I found nothing more than an institution involved in the repetition of practices whose meaning had long been forgotten, but no real connection to something of a genuine spiritual nature. The best of the novices and priests were very simple, good people who were merely content to be able to hide away from the problems of the world.

Before entering the monastery I was known as a most religious fellow, studious and very well behaved; as a result of that experience I became rebellious and started to move away from Catholic Christianity.

Later in life I joined several organizations and individuals engaged in what I called a "spiritual pursuit". One of these organizations was a Protestant Mission, a small crew mainly devoted to the improvement and maintenance of organic human existence. This mission, apart from the predictable opportunists and misfits attracted by this type of organizations, was comprised mostly of enthusiastic, good hearted men, who were very busy trying to help a segment of the Nahua people in central Mexico "improve their living conditions". However, they failed to realize that the Nahua were not, for the most part, interested in our idea of improvement. Thus we were seen more as trespassers trying to impose our own lifestyle than as redeemers.

Concerning a connection with Higher Forces, the leaders of the mission professed to have had a special emotional encounter with the "Lord Jesus Christ", who had endorsed them to engage in such an endeavor. However, they could not explain how it was possible to get this experience, but said that they were chosen. In this sense they were very much like monks, working mostly in the dark but with a strong faith in their mission. They did not believe that any other messiah, saint or savior had the power to provide any kind of salvation or illumination and considered all other spiritual paths and guides as false and misleading. Nothing rare about that, since by now it has become clear that a characteristic of almost anyone following a given creed or spiritual path is the sense of exclusivity. A positive aspect of this is that it keeps people focused working with a common aim; its more dubious feature is the assumption that anyone outside of one's circle is ill-fated.

I must say that during my stay in the mission I never experienced any sort of "emotional encounter with the Lord Jesus Christ". That did not bother me since it did not prevent me from participating in the missionary work itself.

Two issues bothered me constantly, however. First, there was something about this aim of "doing good for its own sake" that I could not quite relate to. It was an external pursuit that merely caused me to feel good about myself, but it did not involve any inner work or change. The other thing that bothered me was that the Nahua people were not exactly thrilled by our presence; since accepting our help also meant accepting our beliefs and lifestyle… under penalty of eternal damnation! I could not take the paradox of us coming to bring a message of hope and help to these people, yet considered everyone who resisted this message as facing eternal punishment. Finally, my leaving the mission was seen as a major tragedy of the sort, since they thought that in doing so, I was putting myself in serious trouble… for all eternity.

You will march in the direction of light, to the east. And in that direction you will shoot your arrows.
                                                    Nahua Song

II

Over the years I tried several possibilities available within my context: groups, studies, and people, but all led to the same dead end. That is, I could not find another person who actually perceived the work of Higher Forces as I did, and they did not reveal the exact nature of my being. I definitely found people who would inspire me to move in a determined direction. Some of them just came and went, leaving me with a message or a reminder; others instead, were part of my life. They possessed a habit or general attitude that represented the clear reminder that my life was not to be taken literally, but as a play.[2]

I remember shortly before I entered the monastery I had this schoolteacher who used to speak to us in riddles. Once he said that no one in the class would ever be able to get the highest mark. "Only God is perfect", he would say, "The highest you can get is a **B**". One day he walked into the classroom, gazed around his class, as if looking for someone in particular, then turned on his heels and wrote the following words (in English) on the blackboard: "*Work when you work, play when you play*". He then fixed his serious eyes on me and asked, "What do you think, Altamirano?" "It is obvious." I said. "You are

---

[2]   When I was a child I wrote a story about finding myself in limbo, where I was given the task of playing the role of Rolando Altamirano, and accepted reluctantly for I knew it was going to be a difficult one.

right. It is obvious", he replied, "but if you observe, you will see you hardly ever do **that**." And without any other explanation he moved on to his lesson. He used to call me "One-eyed-kid," and that did not sound offensive to me. Once during recess I asked him why he kept calling me that. Straight-faced, he replied: "Because in the land of the blind, the one-eyed-man is king," and he walked away.

As my magnetic center developed, I attracted various people who would nourish it, most of the time indirectly. Some of these people appeared to have a magnetic center themselves, because of their discontent with life or their ability to point out the futility of human existence. This ability to see the absurdity of life led them to look for alternative ways of living, and they often ended up in some kind of unconventional lifestyle, which eventually became quite conventional.

Probably the one person who helped me understand this issue was a well known protest singer in exile for whom I worked for five years as a stage hand and secretary when I was eighteen. At the beginning she used to sing mostly social and existential parodies, as well as protest political songs that put her in serious trouble indeed; but soon enough she realized that they did not really make a difference in terms of social change. Later on, using her histrionic genius and charisma, she shifted from a protest singer to a vaudeville show woman, and turned out to be a first-class diva. Most of her songs were inspiring; yet the glamorous lifestyle she inevitably attracted became the very thing she was criticizing in some of them. She was genuinely discontented with the world, and she knew she was of the world. Living with that contradiction made her a very difficult person to work and live with. But I must say she was always very kind towards me. I pictured her as a highly developed being trapped within the laws of ordinary life, and very much in tune with them.

I would need to write a whole document about these people who, in a finely orchestrated way, and under rather unusual circumstances, came into my play and influenced my magnetic center. But for the objective of this text I will only mention one. It was a young man who clearly pointed out the direction that would then lead me to meet and recognize Robert Burton: the embodiment of that which I was meant to remember and be. Before I met this young man who first gave me specific instructions based on esoteric ideas, every effort of mine linked to remembrance of my Self or Higher Forces came only sporadically and in a quite disorganized way.

Also, I will not go into what happened in my life during the time I spent in oblivion; which was essentially the law of accident, just a series of events that could have happened, and do happen in anybody's life at anytime and any place.

"Oz never did give nothing to the Tin Man that he didn't didn't already have".

D. Bunnell

III

Jose Antonio Kahuil was a young Mayan Indian I met while working as a teacher in the Maya zone near the border between Mexico and Guatemala. My encounter with him was rather shocking and, apparently, out of the blue. I was sitting on a bench in the central piazza of the little town I used to live in, quietly smoking and admiring the colorful spectacle of the different Mayan peoples moving around the open space. He approached me for a match, and as I was about to light his cigarette, he removed it from the flame and asked, "How do you spend your time, Sir?" I recognized "something" in the tone of his question and, looking up I noticed a rare gleam in his dark eyes. It made his face look like he was always smiling. He was not looking straight at me, but rather away from me. I lit his cigarette and said, "I live". "Live well, you mean", he replied as he sat down by my side.

I thought that was quite some way to start a conversation with a stranger, but said nothing, intrigued by what he would say next. I felt compelled to listen to the modest tone of his voice, which had a definite effect on me: it changed the quality of my attention. We remained silent for a long time, looking at the passers-by. Finally he said, "Last week, you were sitting right here; your long black hair fell on your shoulders. Today your head is shaved and clean. I almost did not recognize you!" Although I had never seen him before, I did not feel his comment was intrusive or personal at all. I replied with conviction, "I want to see if I remain the same person without my hippy look." He paused for a moment, had a smoke and then remarked, "External change for *esoteric* reasons?" That was the very first time I had heard the word *esoteric* and I did not understand its meaning. I gave him an inquiring look. "*Esoteric* simply means internal", he said, noticing my change of air.

He then told me that he had been observing me for a while before he decided to "enter my life", and that he thought I was not exactly "part of the herd", but fit for a specific kind of work he called *esoteric*. "I am not sure you are the right person for this", he said, "but there is *knowledge* you might be interested in." I could not relate to the statement "enter your life", but I certainly was attracted to the words "there is *knowledge* you might be interested in." Pretending to be thinking, I let some time go by and then asked almost defensively, "What *knowledge* is this?" "Knowledge of your Self", he quietly replied. I experienced mixed reactions as I heard these words, and this was the very first time I heard them. On one hand I **knew** their meaning, and wished to stay connected to this man and find out exactly who he was and what he had to share. On the other hand something within me became diffident and wished to dismiss him, trying to find some flaw in him.

We then went into the formal introductory conversation in which we exchanged the details of our external circumstance, and the reason we happened to live in the same town.

"Ours is not a coincidence."

He came from a small village surrounded by sugarcane plantations, near the coast of southern Mexico. The son of the local medicine man, early in his life he was taught the use of medicinal herbs and substances. He quickly learned to diagnose and apply remedies to such a level that he surpassed his father's skill. This won him the nickname "The Child", since everybody who was in need of his father's services requested "The Child's" opinion on the matter. When I met him, some of his friends and sycophants still referred to him by that nickname, but others who met him later knew him as the "Priest". This nickname was given to him because he was known to have temporarily joined a monastery. This I heard from one of his friends, since he rarely talked about himself. One thing I did hear him say was that he had joined the army for a couple of years. I asked him why he had done such a thing and he replied that he needed to develop will as opposed to willfulness. And when I asked for an explanation of that he said, "Will is of the Self, willfulness is of the body. One has to intentionally put the body in the right circumstances in order to develop certain aspects of the Self." This statement was both appealing and frightening at the same time. The perspective of joining the army in order to develop some inner strength showed that whatever faculty this man possessed, he had acquired through submission. Later on I found the same important principle in Gurdjieff, who stated that a man does not posses real will, but he has enough willpower to put himself under someone else's will, and thus develop real will.

He was a man of very few, carefully selected words. He was very calm too, and remained so even during moments of tension. Whether we were exposed to cold, danger, or the simple irritations of everyday existence, he kept a temperate air.

Although he generally enjoyed himself on a daily basis, Jose Antonio Kahuil seemed to have no attachment to anything in particular. I recall one time he suggested that some of us, including him, set the aim to quit smoking. I was surprised to see that he simply stopped the same day, while I and other people were constantly struggling with it. "How do you do that?" one of us asked. His reply was simple. "Every time I see a cigarette, I say to myself "Not right now, and I obey." I thought this was very clever, since it did not mean "Never again", or "Maybe later", it just meant "not in the moment I get exposed to it". But to obey was his strength.

My first direct question to him was if he had ever perceived the work of Higher Forces in his life. He smiled softly and said, "Did we not say ours is not a coincidence?"

He invited me to join his evening reunions involving a light dinner and "sober drinking". I use this term because I noticed that this man's presence somehow prevented people from becoming intoxicated as we drank steadily. A small group gathered around him; some were his friends, some sycophants who found social advantage in being connected with this very unusual man. It was at these gatherings that I first heard him say, amongst a variety of ideas new to me, that men are governed by planetary influences, and that the glands are the receiving devices of these influences. When asked if it was possible to prove this he replied, "Start with the moon. It is the closest celestial body, and it comes often. See what happens to your mood during the new and the full moon."

He also spoke of the idea that very few people knew about being ruled by the planets, and that fewer tried to overcome their influence; and still fewer succeeded in doing so.

"One who sees the possibility to free oneself from these influences, needs allies, both internal and external", he said. Then he added, "Also, something in us causes us to forget. In order to overcome it we need the help, both of people from the visible world as well as the invisible world." I really appreciated his directness when talking about Higher Forces, whom he used to call "Allies"[3]. This was the very thing that made me stay with him, his ability to read our life from the point of view of Higher Forces helping us out of oblivion. I once pointed out that people who are heedless of Higher Forces are really lost in the world. "On the contrary', he said, 'they are exactly where they belong. It is you and I who are lost; that is why we need to be retrieved."

I do not know where he acquired his knowledge. However he knew most esoteric traditions and used terms from any

---

3   Later on I figured that he had borrowed this term from Carlos Castaneda's account of Don Juan.

of them as he found suitable. Some people thought he was a shaman. I did not think of him that way. I think he was a healer who used hypnosis as a tool to restore people to health. He possessed certain powers, both spiritual and psychological, and a quality of presence that made him seem like he occupied no tangible space… and there was that gleam in his dark eyes. Of course there were also unconscious features in him, as in anybody else, but this paper is not about that.

This man promised never to give me anything I had not already come to by myself. He only arranged my observations according to a system of ideas he possessed. He pointed out an essential fact when I told him that I sometimes saw myself acting and going about my day, doing right and wrong arbitrarily. "What you see is Rolando, not your Self. You have to learn not to confuse one with the other," he stated. This was not very clear for me since at the time I met him my sense of "Self" was mixed up with the body's essence and its most delicate thoughts and emotions, as well as its most intense temporary wants and opinions. In relation to that, he also said: "Rolando is number **one**; YOU are number **two**, and your "Self" is number **three**. Your observation makes you deserving only of **one** and **two**." Although now his words make sense to me, at the time they sounded enigmatic; since they raised the question, "If not the Self, what am I as opposed to Rolando?"

A few times he did use peyote and other substances as tools to show me the different features of my psyche, which he referred to as "your built-in stupidity". I recall him telling me that I had never smoked marijuana. When I assured him that I had, he cheerfully replied, "It probably smoked you. You did not get anything out of the experience other than just getting on and off the merry-go-around." Although at the time I was irritated by his comment, I now see that he meant that there was no aim, or understanding of what I was doing when smoking. It was simply part of my lifestyle as a hippie, a fascinating sensorial experience, sometimes philosophical.

Through the use of these substances he made it possible for me to see at once the series of contradictory thoughts, feelings and actions that constituted my psyche. He did so by stimulating specific associations in my mind as I smoked marijuana or ate mushrooms. Although the experience was painful, he carefully prevented me from getting stuck in a state of paranoia by reminding me that what I was observing was not my Self, but that which prevented me from being my Self.

Yet more importantly he put me in contact with higher centers, the seat of the Self, especially through the use of peyote. He did not just have me ingest the cactus. He took me and others on endless walks into the forest in complete silence, until he decided that we had the right quality of attention required for this practice. He also made it very clear that the plants he used for this purpose were only means to show us both the pitiful state of human existence, as well as man's higher potential. They were not a matter of everyday use: "This is not vitamin for the brain", he would say. "You will have to find a way to get the same results by a sober effort."

In Touch With The Miraculous

A number of people claimed that Jose Antonio Kahuil belonged to some sort of secret brotherhood; maybe so, I do not know. I only remember he once took me with him to visit these Maya "Elders" he was invited to meet. He told me, "You are going to meet the Very Father of these people." He asked me to buy a bottle of expensive brandy and bring it with me as an offering; since I would be allowed to participate in a dancing ceremony with them. Most of it consisted in dancing to an eight note violin tune that went on and on all day long and only stopped for us to have a couple of drinks of their local spirits. Then someone would tell a joke in verse, and as laughter burst out, we started dancing to the same tune again, I ventured to crack a couple of jokes and they were appreciated. This lasted for several days, during which we slept only for a few hours and ate a little once or twice a day. Although during the first day I thought I was going to collapse from drinking and exhaustion, I somehow managed to keep myself together by focusing my attention on the way I related to the music and the two-step dance. At the end of the second day I was in what I described as a "clear state". I now think of it as a higher state. I then noticed that amongst the dancers and musicians, there was a group of six men that always stayed together around these two men, one old and one very young; the old man had the most beautiful face I had ever seen. I can only describe him as "Humility personified". He was so fragile and at the same time so radiant and strong. The men around him seemed to shield him or keep him somehow warm, and they were also different from the rest. They were wearing white headbands and each of them had a walking stick. Noticing my admiration, someone whispered in my ear,

"He liked your gift."

On our way back to our town, Jose Antonio Kahuil asked me what I thought of the experience. He listened to my account with kind attention, and then remarked, "This is just another way to get results".

My relationship with him lasted two years, and ended abruptly when he decided to leave town for an unlimited period of time. He did not ask me or anyone to follow him. He suggested that I buy and read three books: the <u>Bhagavad-Gita,</u> the <u>Tao Te Ching</u> and the <u>Bible</u>, and start from there. He then added that if I decided to lead an ordinary life instead of entering a monastery, I had to find "the game" within the game of life.

Pointing upwards, he said, "They will find it for you."

Shortly after we parted I quit my job as a teacher and set out to find the ideal conditions that would help me practice the knowledge I had learned from this extraordinary man; because I understood by then that I would never be able to get anywhere by myself. I knew I had to find the place where I would be taught what I am, and what I am supposed to do. Strange, is it not?

Jose Antonio Kahuil never spoke of Gurdjieff or Ouspensky, yet he practiced ideas that I later found in them. Some examples are, self-observation as the beginning of work on oneself, or the idea to surrender one's will to someone else if one wishes to develop the willpower necessary to bear a higher state. I did not know anything about the Fourth Way either. In fact, I purchased my first book by Gurdjieff at a street bazaar from a man who heard me speaking about hypnosis, which Jose Antonio Kahuil practiced on a regular basis. This man said that in this book I would find an explanation of that phenomenon. And it was there, the second volume of Beelzebub's Tales to his Grandson that, together with a clear explanation of hypnosis and other impossible explanations, I found a bookmark, with a list of phone numbers. It read "Gurdjieff-Ouspensky Centers".

This unusual book never became my favorite reading, and I was disappointed to learn that Gurdjieff was no longer physically available. I just added him to the list of "allies" helping others become awake; for it seemed to me then that those who are helped out of the limits of human existence are bound to help others escape. Anyway in the bookmark there was the hope that someone like Gurdjieff existed within these "Gurdjieff-Ouspensky Centers".

'Ways' are simply help; help given to people according to their type.

Gurdjieff

IV

The phone numbers in the bookmark I had found in <u>Beelzebub's Tales to his Grandson</u> were obsolete. Every time I called I received the same answer: "This is not the Gurdjieff Ouspensky Center. This is a curtain shop." So I went on to read the books suggested by Jose Antonio Kahuil and found them useful and inspirational, despite the fact that they did not include a practical side. Antonio was not there anymore to explain their esoteric meaning and I always felt that my understanding of them was subjective and, for the most part, literal. In fact this was a major limitation I found when reading esoteric, mystical and philosophical literature, namely, the lack of a living teacher supporting a particular tradition. In this sense I felt that, without Gurdjieff, "Beelzebub's Tales" would remain a mystery.

At the time, Gurdjieff's and Ouspensky's literature in Spanish was hard to find and quite expensive. However I did manage to get a copy of Peter Ouspensky's <u>Talks with a Devil</u>. There was no bookmark in this fine book. Yet in it Ouspensky presented the idea of why the search for something higher was so laborious. As soon as one starts making an effort in that direction something within one awakens to oppose it; yet at that moment I thought Ouspensky was presenting the "devil" as an entity outside of oneself.

Some time later, a friend of mine pointed out an ad in a magazine called "Free Time", with a current phone number of the Gurdjieff-Ouspensky Centers. Little did I know that from the moment I made that call, I would find no "free time" at all. Instead I found a line of effort that would eventually become more and more precise and continuous.

I called and made an appointment for a prospective student meeting and was told to read Ouspensky's book <u>Psychology of Man's Possible Evolution</u>. They suggested a bookstore that carried that and other works by him and Gurdjieff. The very same day I purchased the book I was on my way to the ruins of Palenque, in southern Mexico. I read it all the way there. I must say, I have never found anything as clear and direct as this little work of genius. Everything I had learned from Jose Antonio Kahuil, and more, was presented there in a very simple, practical way. But more importantly, it was expressed in a clear language, as clear and simple as ABC and 123… literally.

As I entered the site of Palenque I went directly to the Temple of the Inscriptions; and I was about to start climbing the stairs when a man stopped me and said, "If you want to see something really special you should follow the path behind the pyramid. Climb to the top of the hill until you see a newly discovered structure." "Really; what is it like?" I asked. "They do not know yet; they are still working on it." He replied.

Curiosity led me around the pyramid where I found the beginning of a path that indeed went uphill. I started walking toward the jungle. As I advanced, the path became more and more difficult to make out, since the jungle became so dense in some places that I could hardly tell the passage of people. Hence, more than tracks on the ground, I began looking for broken branches, trampled bushes and odd shaped trees to help me figure out my way back. At some point the jungle became almost impenetrable, all I could figure out was whether or not I was going uphill. I then realized I could lose my way, and began to make markers.

The silence in the jungle is so strong that it can make one's experience quite eerie, for it is not the silence of a lifeless place, but the silence of latent life, waiting, watching in suspense. I began to feel a bit uneasy and quickened my pace. It was then that I noticed a certain noise other than my own footsteps in the jungle; something like an echo of my own movements. I stopped and turned around; the noise stopped abruptly too. I scanned the jungle and… nothing, not a leaf stirring. Just that silence, a silence as powerful as thunder. I kept climbing, trying to pay attention to the noise I was hearing; perhaps imagining? I then noticed it was coming not from behind me but from my right. "Was this a set up? Was I sent here intentionally so that I would be robbed or something?" My heart started beating fast; but I kept moving uphill, hoping to get to the top and maybe find someone there: some archaeologist or worker. The noise moved to my left, then in front of me, then to my right again. I stopped sharply and with my walking stick moved some bushes aside. I briefly saw the muscular, elegant back of a feline slipping into the jungle, its thick tail barely touching the shrubbery. I became pale with fright as I muttered inside, "That is no monkey." Trying to control myself I looked at my walking stick and held it before me. It looked exactly like a twig.

There was a split second between panic and total control of myself. I took the moment for what it was and calmly pondered my possibilities. I was at least twenty minutes away from the site of Palenque: too far to run or scream for help. Although young and fit, there was no way I could overcome a jaguar. I had nothing with me that could be used as a weapon. Al I had was this fragile walking stick, my belt, and a shoulder bag containing a pen, a notebook and Peter Ouspensky's Psychology of Man's Possible Evolution. I kept climbing, calmer than ever.

What I finally recognized as jaguar-footsteps kept moving around me in circles. Every so often I would see the majestic cat jumping over some small obstacle, but never coming near me. I did not know anything about Jaguars; I just assumed it would sooner or later jump and devour the best of me. I saw this as the moment of my death. I felt strangely calm.

Thoughts were pounding in my head, "What do I have to learn from this? (…) Nothing! This is my last day. I was just supposed to know that there is a way out. Next time I will be able to remember earlier. If Higher Forces are not going to grant me to go on, at least I can accept death without fear." Thoughts like these kept crowding around my troubled spirit. Knowing that the way back to the site was more than twenty eternal minutes long, I decided to move on hoping the summit was just about to appear any moment now.

So I put all of my energies into keeping my aim to get to the top. As the terrain became slightly flat I figured I had arrived to the top of the hill: there was no structure to be seen. I walked around and saw I was just in the middle of the jungle; huge trees reaching way, way up, their foliage covering the sky. Keeping my cool, I started to head back downhill; the jaguar still following me in circles. When I could not see it, I could clearly hear it, and I was constantly expecting the unexpected jump on my back.

Right at the same spot where I first heard it, the jaguar suddenly stopped and went back into the jungle. I felt the impulse to speed up, but refrained and kept walking calmly down toward the site, this time fully aware of myself. When I finally saw the back of the temple of the inscriptions I experienced a genuine feeling of exhilaration. I opened my shoulder bag and took the book out; holding it with both hands. I went to the middle of the site and looked around the neatly built structures… "I wish I could take part in the kind of work that creates such magnificence."

Just then, the man who had pointed out the path approached me and said, "You have been gone for quite a while. When I saw you turning towards the jungle I did not want to stop you because I figured you were just going for a "smoke". I can see you are having a good trip!" "Oh, yes!" I said. "I am so happy to be alive."

"That grass must be good." He winked at me.
"You have no idea."

I want particularly to impress on your minds that the most important ideas and principles of the system do not belong to me.

Ouspensky

V

A couple of weeks later, on Lincoln's birthday, I attended the first of the three "prospective student meetings", as they were called, where the ideas of the Fourth Way were explained. I really appreciated the form of those meetings. The teaching they called the "Gurdjieff-Ouspensky System" was presented in an intentional, orderly, and very clear way. From the first one I realized I had come into contact with a simple, practical teaching. Almost every idea presented could be verified by finding examples in my everyday life. I also felt lucky to have met a group of people who not only "spoke my same language", but who were also working in the same direction in an organized way.

During that first meeting, almost entirely based on Ouspensky's <u>Psychology of Man's Possible Evolution</u>, all participants were advised to explore and verify some of the ideas in our everyday life. For that purpose they gave us a few weeks in between meetings. The main idea I quickly verified was that of sleep. The weeks after the first prospective meeting went by and I did not remember to try to verify the ideas suggested even once. I simply went around my day in a state of elation that sprung from having met these people. But *something* I then called *"the well meaning devil"* prevented me from remembering to verify the ideas. The most important thing was that when I shared my observation at the next meeting, someone pointed out that this was the main reason schools existed, to help one remember. Once more I verified that by myself there is not much I can do, but this organization would help me remember and work on a regular basis.

"This School provides the right conditions for the Work."

Although this was crucial in my decision to join, what made me feel at home was that a considerable number of students saw Higher Forces as the driving energy in their lives and the School. These people came from totally different walks of life and social circumstances and yet they all recognized a series of clearly orchestrated events that led them to join the School. Some of these events bordered on the bizarre, and often touched the miraculous. Of course describing them would require a novelist, or a poet; and I am neither of them. Again, these people knew they had been brought to work together; they were not taught that in the School. So I had finally found not only one, but several people who had verified the work of Higher Forces in their lives and were working together with this understanding. The names given to Higher Forces varied according to the formation of a person's magnetic center: gods, angels, allies, or simply God. In the School they are generally referred to as Influence C.

It was also interesting that they studied cosmic laws from a practical point of view. Thus knowledge that could easily become speculative or even philosophical was turned into an everyday practice. For example, the law of octaves is studied from the point of view of bridging intervals in one's work. That is, while in a descending octave the intervals are bridged mechanically, and the octave simply takes its course; the Work, as it is an ascending octave, requires conscious efforts to bridge intervals. This idea is very practical when one encounters the difficulty of having lost interest or enthusiasm in one's work. It also made perfect sense that the three lines of work in the School are designed to prevent the octave of evolution from deviating. If one comes to an interval in the first line, one still has the second and third lines to engage in some kind of intentional effort to keep moving in the original direction.

It is not my purpose to describe all of the ideas presented at the meetings. I am only describing some that helped me to recognize this as a practical school. Soon enough I understood that this School is not a fixed group of people, but rather a network of individuals within this group of people engaged in the same effort. It was pointed out from the start that this School *"is real only when its participants are real"* - a practical application of Gurdjieff's idea "Life is real only then, when I am". Whenever one is not remembering one's Self or making an effort to remember one's Self, one is not in the School. One becomes like any other person in this planet, engaged in those activities that best suit one's mechanics or organic needs. So whenever any of us engage in an activity that precludes or prevents the Work, we are simply part of a festival of fools. From the beginning the School was presented as being esoteric, invisible, and noticeable only by one who is remembering one's Self or who is attempting to remember one's Self.

Time in the School is not measured in years, but in one's ability to be present.

The second prospective meeting was presented with the aid of an ordinary deck of cards that explained certain aspects of the infrastructure of the human machine. It was like a map of what in the teaching is called "the lower functions". This map is very helpful for classifying the different observations of the multiplicity of I's. Not every "I" produced in one is of the same nature. They are classified as intellectual, emotional, moving or instinctive. I's coming from the sex center were not explained at that meeting. And higher emotional and higher intellectual were described as dormant.

The concept of sleep is connected to higher centers.

Many new practical ideas sprung from this meeting. One was the idea of attention. They described the human machine as capable of working on three different levels of attention, namely: uncontrolled and scattered, controlled by an event, and controlled by effort. The latter is largely encouraged in the School due to the fact that it puts one in the position to divide one's attention. In fact, most of the School's meetings and events require one to develop kings of centers, or controlled attention. Divided attention, a characteristic of Self Remembering, is entirely the responsibility of the individual.

Now, in relation to controlled attention, we were advised

to take heed of the work of the intellectual part of the instinctive center, or king of clubs, as this part of the machine is the one that controls all others. It manipulates the work of all the other functions and can simulate it if necessary. The fact is that as one makes the effort to be in kings of centers or controlled attention with the aim to awaken higher centers, one can observe that the king of clubs becomes active and tries to make the experience part of its territory. Ouspensky's little devil was a hint of this occurrence.

Another concept that I found essential is that every machine is born with one of the lower functions more developed than the others, and that this function affects the way one sees the world when higher centers are asleep. This is called the mechanical center of gravity. It is necessary to find it; and simultaneously try to develop (by will) a center of gravity based on the Work, which would help one remember one's Self more often. This center of gravity is in the king of hearts, or emotional intelligence. From this level of controlled attention one is encouraged to create a deputy steward and, eventually, a steward. Thus the king of hearts was presented as the narrow gate that leads one to higher centers. This idea explained my higher experiences with Jose Antonio Kahuil, and put a finger on my question, "What am I as opposed to Rolando?" In the System this is called the steward.

The steward is not an inherent part of the machine. It has to be created by will to assist the awakening of higher centers.

The third prospective meeting was about the human machine in connection to the cosmos above organic life on earth, that is, the solar system. It included a description of every human type. Seven glands rule human behavior, and in each person the work of one gland prevails over the others. This gives rise to a specific mechanical tendency called chief feature. Every human machine tends to act and react constantly from this chief feature, even when circumstances require him to act differently.

I had heard from Jose Antonio Kahuil about the theory of planetary influences and human glands as receptors of such influences; and about the possibility to escape them, but he never mentioned how. At this meeting a hint was given as to how to free oneself from planetary influences. It started with the suggestion to engage in the methodical observation of one's machine from the point of view of how to control its chief feature and center of gravity regardless of what planetary influences are affecting one in the moment. The discovery of one's type was the first step.

Additionally, one of the students, an astronomer, had been assigned the task to follow the motion of the planets and meteor showers, as well as the appearance of solar storms, and to provide the School with a monthly almanac of such influences; just like the ancient Toltec schools used to do in their so called calendars.

They also explained that "photographing" each other's mechanics played a great part in this endeavor, for others could see one from different perspectives. Needles to say, it took several years of trial and error before I could discover my machine's type, chief feature, and center of gravity. And it is taking forever to find ways to neutralize their manifestations. Yes, this is a never ending endeavor since the chief features of the machine are built-in devices. Therefore they remain there for life.

Fragments Of An Enduring Teaching

The possibility of receiving C Influence must be limited because if one does not make use of it, what is the good of wasting it?

Ouspensky

VI

At the end of the third prospective meeting, which was very short, we were told about the School in general, including the donations necessary for its growth and maintenance. That was a problem for some, but it made perfect sense to me since by then I had participated in several organizations that depended solely on the efforts and means of their members. In short, from the beginning I understood that the School was "a potluck dinner" where everyone invited had to bring in whatever their means allowed. Of course there is a minimum amount one is supposed to produce monthly. This requisite is based on one of the main ideas of the System which states that, in the Fourth Way, work on oneself begins at the level of a good householder.

"The work of each person may involve expenses, traveling and so on. If his life is so badly organized that a thousand rubles embarrasses him, it would be better for him not to undertake this work. Through our demand we find out whether he is able to work with us or not." Gurdjieff

Also, during this last meeting, space was given for questions regarding the teaching and the School. My first question was "Who is the teacher?" I was told that his name was Robert Burton, that he lived in California, and that I could meet him only after a year of working in the center. I became impatient, but was told I had a year to learn to wait. In the meantime I started reading and translating the words of the teacher, Robert Burton. And I produced a journal in Spanish based on translations of his thoughts.

For a while I thought that was as close as I could get to him during that year. And it was close enough for I realized that this man kept saying the same thing over and over, "Remember Your Self." Ouspensky had previously pointed out that "Self Remembering" is the hub of this System, and Robert Burton kept on tapping into this. Robert focuses on the Self that has to be remembered.

I also realized that this man spoke of truths I had known since the beginning of time. He stated facts I knew as a child but was unable to articulate; he practiced ideas I knew as an adolescent but was too distracted to hold on to. He was able to point out **the essential** and present it in an orderly and refined whole. Like an ibis, he accurately plucked the truth from the mud of imagination and fed it to its hatchlings.

Moreover, something else came into sight in the meantime. One could clearly perceive that the people who regularly visited us from the heart of the School in Northern California had been exposed to a distinctive kind of influence and work. They were very different from traveling students and teachers who came to visit from centers other than the heart of the School, where Robert Burton lived. I once mentioned this to one of them, Walter, who acknowledging my observation, told me with a smile, "Yes, we are running on his fuel for now. If you want to accumulate the same hydrogen and crystallize it within you, you have to make continuous, organized efforts."

Finding the School has nothing to do with finding a group of people who share the same ideals. Instead, it means to find a specific line of action *some* of these people are engaged in, and what is more, to find a group of people brought and kept together by a higher intelligence. Now, in order to connect to this higher intelligence one needs to awaken higher centers; there is no other way. If someone is trying to wake up your higher centers and you do not make the effort to awaken, your lower self will only make their efforts part of its dreams or nightmares.

Among the people in the center at the time, there was one particular person to whom I was drawn from the start. Thanks to repetition, everybody had a good grip on the ideas, but this person had a special ability to think in terms of verifying every idea of the System.

Ms. Goldstein was a psychologist, but more than anything she was a compassionate person. She gave me the impression of being a four year old genius playing in the field of the human psyche, very simple and almost naïve in the way she read human behavior. This innate ability to read people's behavior, together with a sound understanding of the System, made her a great teacher-figure. While others in the center mostly shared their personal observations in the Work, she focused on trying to prove how the ideas of the System entered every aspect of one's life, and how every major idea required the effort to divide attention. She did this successfully keeping herself out of the picture. I did not realize at the time the meaning of our relationship, but later on I understood that our conversations had been essential in my development of a deputy steward. There was no question or problem that I introduced in our conversations which did not lead to self observation and the classification of my mechanics in terms of the System.

In fact, thanks to her instruction I engaged in the first serious invisible efforts and actually saw the results of those efforts. I will only mention one particular example to illustrate how this happened. It was a very powerful experience, and it led me to a further, devastating verification.

The story goes that when I joined the School, I invited my close friends and relations to attend the prospective student meetings. I even wrote a letter to Jose Antonio Kahuil giving him the news (Many months later he replied in his usual puzzling way: "Remember Oliver Twist? His difficulties begin when he asks for more.") Anyway, the only person to join the School was my partner. All went well for a while, until she started to get involved with someone else in the center. The way we found out was unexpected and quite shocking.

The first interesting thing about this shock was that although the center was very small and young at the time and everybody was well aware of the matter (and to a certain degree disturbed by it) our meetings never lost their focus and fine energy. Their form remained intact regardless of the tension created by the affair; for we were all part of the same School and we all had to work with the situation *beyond* the best of our abilities, *beyond* our morality and most tender feelings.

To begin with, the fact that people took my side was described by Ms. Goldstein as a good example of the law of feminine dominance[4]. My finding her observation outrageous simply proved that she was right. And, as I see now, she was right. That was the first time I experienced this law operating within me. According to our local morality, these two people had done something very wrong that called for some sort of punishment. Yet from the point of view of a higher aim we all shared, the focus had to be on the great opportunity this shock represented in terms of self study and self control. So basically I had to feel lucky.

Ms. Goldstein's mind was so agile that she used this opportunity to help me put into practice the basic ideas of the System. The main one was to see negative emotions as higher hydrogen which could be transformed into Self Remembering. At some point I asked her, "What is the right effort to apply now?" "Well", she said, "Try to see your Self as **separate** from Rolando. Every time **you** succeed in not expressing negativity, and see it as higher hydrogen, **you** can experience your Self." That was a very good and difficult way to put it. I practiced it as much as I could; trying to hold on to that new understanding like a

---

4   Feminine Dominance is the law that keeps people within the boundaries of conventional behavior.

board in the middle of the ocean. This was also the first time I verified what it meant to apply the first conscious shock; that is, to try not to express negative emotions and separate from them. Applying the second conscious shock or transforming negative emotions depended on the success of that first effort.

Ms. Goldstein was a thoughtful person, and very professional. She did not take sides in the whole matter; she simply worked with everyone involved in private. Although I do not know what she told other people, in the end it was suggested that my now former partner should make official her new relationship and I would have to move on with my work.

That experience was agonizingly humiliating; and it seemed never to come to an end, since we all met several times a week and worked on second and third line together. So I basically got to witness this affair and work with my reactions. Whenever I did not succeed in my efforts, the instinctive center simply found ways to eliminate the energy produced within the machine. It did this in various forms, such as poetry writing, rage, and gossip about the people involved in its suffering.

Applying the System ideas at this time was like fighting an invisible force in the dark, but I trusted Higher Forces, and Ms Goldstein, and I verified that the System worked. Several weeks later I came to experience the awakening of higher centers, something of the same nature I came across when I ate peyote with the assistance of Jose Antonio Kahuil. It is a calm, wordless state where one witnesses existence as a game, or a stage. One does not attach one's identity to anything happening in the moment, within or without oneself. Yet while peyote had provided this result in a matter of minutes (though also great nausea) this time it had taken me weeks of sleepless nights and endless days trying to separate from the most violent thoughts and emotions.

That was also the time when an extraordinary incident took place within my body. I was lying in bed one night, unable to sleep, tired and stressed out from trying to stop the same painful recurring thoughts and images. I suddenly felt my whole body start to shiver with freezing cold and yet burning. Some energy was moving up and down me as if I was being scrubbed. Then all of a sudden a white light, like thunder, exploded through my forehead, leaving a slight pulsation that lasted for quite some time. I stayed in bed for a while, curious to see what would come next. Nothing did. I felt sober and strong. The negative emotions I had been trying to separate from for the last month or so were not there anymore; I was in a neutral state. I looked around the room. Although it was still dark, I sensed the first indication of dawn. I lay in bed, feeling grateful. When the light finally unveiled the room, I got up and went for a walk around the beautiful neighborhood where we used to live. It was a lovely morning. I had come to be what I was looking for, and although the trial and effort required to achieve that were no small things, I was grateful that I had finally appeared. However something within me was totally frightened. Although I knew who it was, I did not call it "the lower self" then.

From that moment on, my aim became to learn to retrieve that state and make it permanent, but the lower self became increasingly active with the intention to curb my efforts.

I remembered then that Higher Forces must arrange circumstances in one's life that will produce enough friction and energy for higher centers to manifest; the reason being that in general one is not able to produce enough friction at will. Once one has experienced the tremendous struggle to transform suffering, one's lower self will make every effort not to let that happen again. So Higher Forces have to use the machine's tendencies and identifications in order to produce what we call a "play of friction." Plays of friction are not meant to cleanse one, or to help one change the machine's behavior; one is not expected to become good but to transform the energy produced by these plays. And the effort to produce higher centers during a play of friction depends exclusively on one. One has to put forth all of one's will against the machine's mechanical reactions; because while (in this case) the machine claims "justice", "punishment" etc, the divinity within simply struggles to appear and be.

Sometimes, however, such plays of friction can be the result of accident, or fate, or cause and effect. It is all the same for one who wants to awaken. One must profit from them in the same way nonetheless.

Yet Ms Goldstein, with all of her inner beauty and wisdom, did not *understand* the very principles she had so laboriously and lovingly instilled in me. A number of years later she went through a similar play –or rather worse. Her partner left her for another student in the center, creating the very same inner atmosphere as the one I had gone through. I was shocked to see that there was no way she could think in terms of the System then, she did not have the will to transform or separate from negativity; or to apply any of the ideas she had so encouraged me to make practical. She simply started to sink in one negative emotion after another, until she finally faded away from the School; and later on, from the Center. It was a devastating verification of the difference between knowledge and being: To see my counselor, who inspired me and helped me in a very loving and organized way, not wanting to hear the same in relation to herself. All she wanted was "off with his head!" And she was right, she was terribly right; however as Ouspensky said in relation to negativity, "so much the worse if you are right."

One last thing to add is that this was not the only time I encountered this particular "play of friction". For a reason then obscure to me but now evident, I kept attracting the same play over and over for more than ten years (always linked to relationships) until I was able to neutralize the mechanics that caused me to engage in that particular waste of energy. I remember asking the Teacher at some point why I had to have the same kind of friction time and again. As I recall he said, "Higher Forces want you to internalize your efforts." I must say it took many years of neutral observation and help both from Higher Forces and the School before I was in the position to change something internally; and though this mechanics is still latent, it remains passive. As pointed out before, one does not get rid of some mechanics once and for all. More exactly one develops the will necessary to control them. There is essentially nothing wrong with mechanics. They are part of the cosmic plan. It is just that in the Fourth Way, one's mechanics are turned into tools to awaken higher centers.

Even now, every time these mechanics emerge I have to make much effort to control them, though it is certainly not as excruciating.

Nobody can get any sleep, there's someone on everybody's toes.

R. Zimmerman

VII

Soon after I joined we were asked to rent a house, not just an apartment, but a real house: preferably with a garden or some sort of facility that would allow for third and second line octaves. That was called a "Teaching House" because our meetings and events were held there, but mainly because only Fourth Way students could live in it. Several of us volunteered to move in and take care of the rent and utilities. This is a very good example of third line. Namely, members of the School have to provide the circumstances that create opportunities for working on three lines of work. The Teaching Houses are a very good example of what esoteric School is about. We create a space, a circumstance, as a team. It belongs to nobody and it serves all. In other words "Teaching Houses" are nobody's home, yet they are everybody's space for work. Rules and exercises are provided by the Teacher and every individual is responsible to practice them internally.

This is an especially helpful environment for learning to work on oneself, since one is totally immersed in the School. It helps one to refocus in one's work after a day of interacting with people not related to it. I moved in without hesitation.

An important function of these Teaching Houses has been, on one hand, to learn to control one's behavior in relation to people, and conversely, to learn to live with their unpleasant manifestations. In other words, to learn to live together regardless of our unavoidable differences, because we know we need each other as constant reminders and support for the Work. The Teacher once said that he did not call them "Houses of Friction" because if he did, nobody would want to move in. In the Teaching House one has to be alert if one wants to learn something.

Similarly, Apollo is everybody's space for work, but it is nobody's property.

Of course every once in a while Higher Forces would throw into the Teaching House a trouble-maker, often even unrelated to the Work, just to add to the pressure. In general, apart from each individual's interest in the Work, there is hardly any affinity in terms of personality or essence among those living in a Teaching House. And when there is affinity, it often leads to distraction.

Every teacher, or guru, is a specialist in some one thing.
Gurdjieff

VIII

After reading accounts of Gurdjieff and Ouspensky by people who actually met them, it became clear to me that Gurdjieff's mechanical center of gravity was the moving-instinctive, and that his teaching was based on that function. Ouspensky's instead, was the intellectual center and his teaching also took the character of that particular center. Robert Burton is centered in the emotional center, so the form of our School is based on that function. In fact, his teaching was described to me as "The Art of Living." So Robert does not teach through sacred dances like Gurdjieff did. He does not request that we try to think as if we were already conscious. His meetings are not based on a question-answer format, like Ouspensky's. Robert created a social form that would require us to learn to live together, and work together on a long term basis as friends, bearing with others weaknesses and trying to control our own. This last phrase might sound easy and even ideal, but it has proven to be one of the most difficult tasks ever required from a human being. Unlike friendships in life, friendships in the School are not mechanical. They require constant conscious effort.

As part of the form of Robert's teaching we were asked to organize formal dinners, trips to museums and ballet performances, listen to the finest classical music and read the greatest classical literature. In short, we were asked to surround ourselves with beautiful, refined impressions, as a way to provide our essence with finer hydrogen as we divide attention. That is a very attractive aspect of the form of the School, for one gets exposed to the best in every culture. As a byproduct, throughout the years, many people all over the world received an education that they would not have pursued if left to their own devices.

Additionally the form of the School's gatherings (primarily meant to serve as a background for Robert's teaching; but also to provide the conditions for the three lines of work to take place) is actually very hospitable to a newcomer and rather glamorous. The dress code is elegant. Conversation is kept on a high level, with a subject intentionally chosen and dealt with. There is a very graceful atmosphere, often involving servers and ushers wearing tuxedos, food and wine of the best quality. From outside it looks like a series of high society gatherings. Over the years this has attracted many people not necessarily interested in the Work, but mainly fascinated by its form. These people come, enjoy themselves for a while, get bored of it, and drift away.

What remained unnoticed at the beginning is the amount of money, planning and effort it takes to put all of this together. All food and setting preparation, dish and pot washing, as well as the clearing of the setting late at night are done by students who in general do not have an affinity for the task, but do it voluntarily.

As for most students who play the role of guests and donors, the form of the School's events is so foreign that to attend them is always a great effort. The lifestyle projected in them is certainly not very comfortable for most of us who have come from backgrounds different from this one. Therefore most students' instinctive centers feel constrained wearing elegant clothes, talking to people they hardly know, and having to behave in a congenial way. To attend an event takes an effort to be in kings of centers, or control one's attention even from the moment one is getting ready for it.

More than often one has to drag one's lower self to an event. Having observed this; I once asked the Robert how he managed to attend all those events, since he always has to be there. As I recall it he said, "The machine has limitations that the third eye does not have."

In Touch With The Miraculous

Deep can only call to deep.

Christina Rossetti

IX

At the beginning one may find it relatively easy to think of everyone involved in the School as a friend in the Work. In time, the inevitable happens: friendships based on mechanics start to develop; tensions based on mechanics start to develop. In short, all kinds of unconscious interactions possible within the context of human society start to develop; and almost none of these tendencies is related to the Work; such as sexual attractions, friendships and enmities based solely on habits or features…ghettos based on nationality, race or social status.

It took a long time of self observation before some of us could realize that not all of our interactions with the people in the School were related to the Work, especially those gatherings outside the center or the form of the School. It became then necessary to separate the School from its body, which is called "The Fellowship of Friends"; one must not confuse one with the other because neither of them is what it seems.

One has to be selective and choose the right people and circumstances that do encourage one's work. For just as very few I's produced in the machine are related to the Work, very few people in the School are actually connected to the Work at a given moment. The fact being that tendencies related to the Work are not mechanical at all. That is, the tendency to divide attention, to remember one's Self, to create an observing "I", to develop a steward, to remind each other of the Work. These tendencies remain a moment to moment struggle. Everyone in the Fellowship influences one's mechanics, few influence one's work.

Oftentimes I have to go through the painful process of walking out on a friendship or relationship that starts to become some sort of mutual gratification, nothing connected to the Work. The most painful of all remains my breaking up with Ms Goldstein.

Everyone is in great need of one particular exercise, both if one wants to continue and for external life.
                                        Gurdjieff

X

Since the beginning we were given a series of "exercises" to introduce during the day. They have been very useful over the years to help us exercise controlled attention and develop will.

Different evolutionary ways use different exercises and techniques to develop will and attention: fasting, prayer, dancing, breathing exercises or exercises for the mind. All of them are, so to speak, artificial activities. They often have nothing to do with one's organic needs, and sometimes even go against one's nature. Now, because this is the Fourth Way, and it takes place in life, exercises have to be based on ordinary life's activities, thus invisible. We have exercises related to eating, drinking, speaking, sex, human relations, etc. Most of them look like nothing special; they are based on common sense and good manners. Some examples are: wearing a seatbelt while driving, refraining from interrupting while someone else is speaking, or from sex outside of marriage.

Some of these exercises have become permanent (the one's directly connected to the form of the School and the development of attention in the emotional center) but most of them are changed as they become mechanical habits.

"Our exercises require Self Remembering."

On the other hand one can observe how the king of clubs takes exercises literally, as rules it has to follow to be acceptable in terms of the form of the School. Sometimes it goes as far as making an exercise part of its psychological makeup or lifestyle, to the point that, in sleep, it tends to become the law enforcement officer of this or that exercise. In other cases it tries to oppose exercises thinking that avoiding them does not harm its idea of evolution.

There are many wrong ways to relate to exercises, but they are all designed for Self Remembering and the development of attention in the moment.

Apart from exercises, the Teacher offers suggestions and tasks on a personal level, which are based on direct observations of his students' mechanics. Some of these suggestions and tasks are easy to work with, others instead, put one face to face with the enemy within.

In order to be true, the teaching must be one of many. If it is unique, it means it is invented.

Ouspensky

XI

I did not know anything about the Fourth Way or the System until a week or so before I attended the introductory student meetings. Therefore I did not know of the existence of any other Gurdjieff-Ouspensky schools or groups. I deem myself lucky on this issue since I came with a fresh and open mind both to the System and to the School. Apart from Jose Antonio Kahuil, I did not have a way to compare the Work in this School with others': I simply saw that students worked along the same lines as Jose Antonio Kahuil had directed me, so I started working with them.

Later on I learned that there are other schools and institutions linked to the Work as staged by Gurdjieff or Ouspensky. They claim they are the righteous heirs to Gurdjieff's teachings, and some of them have questioned the authenticity of our School. It has been pointed out that the sense of exclusiveness is inherent in most people pursuing a spiritual path, but this has never affected anybody else's Work on a daily basis.

There is no way of telling if Higher Forces work with other people; a short story by Alejo Carpentier, "The Chosen"[5], illustrates my understanding on this issue. On the other hand, spending time questioning the legitimacy of someone else's efforts is a deviation and a waste of

5   His book is called "War of Time."

precious time.

When I joined the School I saw that the efforts encouraged and required from one are esoteric, and that the practices are linked to the awakening of higher centers: and what is more, I verified that real efforts lead to real results. There is no discipline in the School which is not linked to the necessity to develop a special kind of attention; all disciplines require Self Remembering.

The main factor that keeps this School together is that most people have verified the work of Higher Forces in their lives long before meeting the teaching or Robert Burton, and we keep verifying their influence on a daily basis. We know that the System was given to us, and we were given each other to work together. We recognized this when we joined.

On the other hand, one who learns about Higher Forces from the School without personally verifying them is destined to either deny their existence or to relate to them in a credulous way, and to think of them in terms of their own organic needs.

I will speak whatever you put within my heart; only that will issue forth from my lips.

Huehuehtlahtolli

XII

During the year I spent in the center, we received visits from a network of students traveling around the world. These students had a certain amount of experience in the Work, and of course, knew the ideas well. They played the role of figure-teachers for new ones. Some of them turned out to be remarkable in their explanation of the ideas and in their ability to turn situations into work opportunities. Throughout the years the number of such traveling students has increased and quite a few of them have become remarkable teachers of the Fourth Way.

The role of a teacher-figure is risky. Although it puts a certain amount of pressure on one's first line, one has to bear in mind that the System is not one's own, nor the form in which one is facilitating its assimilation. It is vital to keep in mind that one's role is a vehicle for the work of Higher Forces. Moreover, when one passes on the message one has to strive to BE the essence of that message. Otherwise the lower self is just taking this role personally while being used to disseminate the teaching. Generally speaking the ideas are easy to absorb and remember due to constant repetition. What remains a struggle is to put them into practice.

These ideas are not one's own. Only one's conscious efforts to apply them are.

The order of the small world is the image of that of the great world.

Ibn Gabirol

XIII

A year went by and I was ready to travel to California and meet Robert Burton. By that time I had read several accounts, both of Gurdjieff and of Ouspensky, so I fancied Robert Burton to be at least like one of them. Later I found out I guessed right, but I did not know which one of the two and in which way.

Before actually visiting the heart of the School, at the time called Renaissance[6], I visited the various centers in California. There I received my first cultural shock within the School. I saw that its form takes a different character depending on the culture wherein it materializes. I will not go into detail about this; think of it as going to another country and verifying that they brew their coffee in a totally different way than Mom did. This was very helpful in the process of learning to differentiate the form of the School from the School itself. When I came to California I verified that the School was here; the form of the School was here too, but with a slightly different flavor.

A number of years later, after living in different centers in Europe, Mexico and the USA, and of course, Renaissance I learned to make the distinction between the School, and the Fellowship of Friends. The Fellowship of Friends is the body, the School the work of Higher Centers within the body.

---

6   It used to be called "Via del Sol", later on "Isis" and nowadays it is called "Apollo."

In Touch With The Miraculous

The Fellowship is a collection of people working together with a common aim; the School is its invisible Presence: a sacred atmosphere.

Additionally, the Fellowship of Friends exists within organic life on earth, and attracts all kinds of people not always related to esoteric work (even though they create opportunities for the Work). Even though the School remains open to every individual who enters its field of influence, not everybody who joins the Fellowship is destined to receive this influence.

It has been pointed out that the School can only be seen and understood by one who is either in a higher state, or trying to reach a higher state.

In the second state, all one encounters is the Fellowship of Friends, and one is bound to focus on its external form and mechanical aspects, which are of the exact same nature as those in any other organization involving human beings. All six cosmic processes take place within the Fellowship, and only one of them is conscious in nature. The rest we have learned to deal with to the best of our abilities.

Nothing is given by God, only Nature gives.
                                    Gurdjieff

XIV

The first time I ever traveled to the heart of the School with the aim to meet Robert Burton I did not make it there. I had arrived through San Francisco and spent a few days in the center. The car that was supposed to drive us there broke down a few miles south of Sacramento, and we had to spend the night in a motel. (In those days the trip to Renaissance from the bay area was sort of an odyssey.) When the car was ready it was time for the student who drove me to go back to work in San Francisco. So I had to wait for another week until someone else drove me there the following weekend. As I arrived at Renaissance, I learned that Robert Burton was traveling.

While in San Francisco I met a very gentle student who had been appointed by Robert as what in the System is called a "Man Number Five". He made a strong impression on me as someone truly kind and attentive, but I did not perceive any more than that. However, the fact that he had been appointed by the Teacher made me think that probably I did not really know what exactly a man number five was; plus, people treated him with special respect. A few months later this student left the School and started a group of his own, taking along those who wanted to follow him. I was somewhat disappointed by the whole matter, but a student properly pointed out that one could not rely one's own efforts on anybody else's, man number five or not.

As years went by, I noticed that every once in a while Robert would appoint certain students as prominent in terms of the teaching, and they become figure-teachers for new students for a while. I am inclined to envision these roles as tests; having observed the tendency in the machine to bury real efforts under a role of service and take the teaching personally.

When a new person arrives with his luggage, he is at once undressed... This is why those among you who do not know about this get the impression that we have collected here only people who are stupid, lazy, dense; in a word all the riff raff.

Gurdjieff

XV

My job as a teacher allowed me to spend the summer in California, so when I decided to visit the heart of the School I knew it would be for an extended period. I immediately made arrangements to become part of the permanent working crew and was gladly welcomed. There were some hundred and fifty students working there at the time, mostly Americans. One could tell that a number of them had sprung from the sixties hippie movement.

The focus of third line work then was in the vast vineyard that had been carved into a series of slopes ten years before or so and in the building of a winery. Of course there were many other octaves available but the vineyard was the major one. I was considered fit for the vineyard crew, which was rather small, divided in departments. Mine included three people, and apart from harvests and octaves that required all hands on deck, we worked mostly alone. One of my first assignments was to dig the holes for the trellis in one of the newest slopes overlooking the Sierra Nevada Mountains. So I had to start from the top and, as weeks progressed, I found myself at the bottom of the slope.

This third line octave became an intense experience, since I was told that a bear had been spotted in that area, and I just needed to be aware of that. I became apprehensive every time I was dropped off at the top of the slope and started walking downwards. I used to jump at the slightest little noise I heard or imagined to hear. I recall a clear moment of wonder when I got to the bottom of the slope and found a half eaten deer! I asked a question at a small meeting on how to work with this potentially dangerous situation. Someone suggested a very interesting line of effort. As I recall they said: "Though you have to know how to behave in the event of an encounter, you cannot deal with the bear until you actually see it. Fear is in the moment. The main work is with imagination." Needless to say I never saw the bear back then, (the first one I actually saw was at my back door a couple of days ago), but I learned a few techniques to stay out of imagination. The most effective one was the looking exercise.

Robert Burton was away and I did not see him for the first few weeks. So I spent my time getting acquainted with the people at Renaissance. I noticed that, apart from the code of behavior at events, some people's conduct was, in general, loose and free, often even wild. A friend of mine told me that in the centers the School was pretty much connected to the form, and that essence experienced the Work through true personality. At Renaissance essence was in direct contact with the School, so it was necessary to be true to oneself, and not as one thought others expected one to be in terms of the form of the School, otherwise one would never be able to know oneself and be one's Self. This friend of mine was quite an unconventional person, but true to himself. Even when he left the School, he told me that after years of work he had not seen any results and that he would just have to move on: but he did not blame anybody for that.

Soon I discovered that many students at Renaissance seemed somehow unconventional in terms of the form of the School, different from those who came to visit on weekends and on holidays. The simple reason was that everybody lived day to day, hour to hour and minute to minute in a foreign environment. There were people from all kinds of backgrounds and nationalities. Even amongst the American students, no one was a native of the location chosen to build the heart of the School, and almost no one was trained to perform the tasks needed to clear and develop the land.

Students were left to their most mechanical devices and their own ability to control them.

I certainly am not a farmer or a gardener, and was born and raised in one of the warmest climates on the planet, close to the "City of Eternal Spring". So basically this place has always been too cold and wet in the winter, too hot and dry in the summer, and the spring lasts only a few weeks! I was used to books, classrooms and typewriters, and here I was given a posthole digger, a shovel and a pair of clippers as my work tools. For many years voluntary suffering remained the focus of my work; which essentially meant to force my machine out of bed in the morning, and be ready to face the freezing rain in the winter or the scorching sun in the summer. It was back then that I developed the impulse to start working on myself at dawn, just before I opened my eyes.

We worked six days a week, from dawn to dusk, and were so exhausted at the end of the day that I hardly had any energy left for reading or writing. We did have meetings and live concerts with world class musicians during the week, but some of us were so tired that we spent the whole concert trying to avoid going into first state. We lived in this place in the middle of nowhere, away from the world. The ambiance back then was very similar to that of a monastery way up in the mountains.

At the time I arrived there was hardly any place to stay. Some of us slept on the lawns surrounding the newly built structures during the summer. In winter one could sleep on the floor in the different rooms of the Renaissance Town Hall, usually under a piano, until one finally found a permanent place to stay. In my case, one of the few students who owned a home put a bed in a little shed in the back of his house, and a shelf with an old lamp on it. He let me stay there until I found something more civilized.

All of these conditions were very propitious for the emergence and nourishment of essence. The nourishment of essence was provided mostly by the exercises and the form of the School, all of which constitute what in the System is called true personality. However, the emergence of essence brought into play a different kind of game. Namely it brought us to the verification, with all its consequences, of Gurdjieff's remark: *"As a rule a man's essence is primitive, savage and childish, or simply stupid."* What Gurdjieff did not mention in his remark is that not only essence is immature, but often damaged, and at times irreversibly so.

Some students still managed to have true personality as the third force in their daily interactions, especially those with roles of responsibility. Yet after a while, others simply started to act from essence. This created circumstances, conflicts and troubles which caused many people to think that we were not a real school. Although most of that turmoil is gone by now, it was a very successful phase in the School because it helped many of us start working directly from essence. Almost no one was under the law of feminine dominance of their original social herd; everybody had a lot of rope to do whatever they liked. Most students discovered that essence is not interested in the Work. It pursues whatever makes it feel genuinely satisfied, which makes it a perfect target for the lower self. The tasks and exercises designed to educate essence were points of reference which no one was going to actively enforce. Apart from being photographed, no one could really be helped. The education of essence depended solely on the strength of the individual's own will. Only self observation brought one to understand one's essence; only Self Remembering could monitor its mechanical manifestations. But for several years all one could do was observe and try to remain neutral towards oneself and towards others. When one did not succeed in this, one had to just try again.

My focus then was the creation of will, and it only meant

to observe impartially, without changing anything. This required patience both from me and especially from others. Results were proportional to right effort, and they were internal.

Of course some essences posed no complications to this particular social environment. Say a Saturn-Mars, king of hearts would be mechanically well behaved; a jack of clubs in charge of the gardens would be a well-liked individual. But a Venus-Mercury queen of hearts fond of song, sex and wine, would be, in general, more of a "trouble maker."

*Unfortunately C influence very often becomes B
influence if people come to a school unprepared.*
Ouspensky

XVI

Because the School is in life, over the years we have tried different ways to make it available to people with the right magnetic center. However we inevitably attract people totally unrelated to the Work. Some join because they are sincerely dissatisfied with life and want to find a place that provides a shelter from their disillusion. Some are pure misfits, others opportunists, or even emotionally religious people. Yet others join simply because their mom or their boyfriend brought them. Some people confuse the School with the Fellowship of Friends at Apollo, which at times appears to be a cordial alternative community, and they wish to blend into its folklore for a while. (Other times this community seems a bit rowdier than "Macondo"[7].)

In short, this School has an external form that also attracts people unable to profit from it. After enjoying the form and folklore of the Fellowship for a while, these people leave, sometimes in groups. Some leave when they become more balanced and are capable of finding a better job or a relationship. In general people leave when they find out that they can get somewhere else what they were looking for here.

Those who never developed any kind of discipline before

---

7   "Macondo" is the town around which revolves "<u>A Hundred Years of Solitude</u>" a novel by Garcia Marquez.

joining the School will find it very difficult to profit from it.

Another type of people attracted to the School is usually passive in relation to the Work. That is they tend to believe in the School as an organization outside of themselves which is supposed to produce some kind of "state of grace" or "something" by simply belonging to it. After a few weeks, or months or years of "nothing happens" they blame it on the Teacher and the School and then leave, as a rule, resentfully.

It is fair to leave if after a while one does not see results, but one cannot blame it on anyone. The School can only provide the right circumstances for the Work; one's success depends solely on one's own aims and efforts.

Of course there have been students who at the beginning, were focused and engaged in serious inner work; they achieved results and understood the nature of the School. These specific students usually came to a point in their work where they met a denying force they had not foreseen, that is they had to let go of some kind of major weakness or blindness… or a major identification[8]. The process of letting go of such identification is usually painful and it may take a long time. Having gone through a couple of such episodes, I can say that one has to be ready to go insane for a while until one regains one's balance in the Work again. Otherwise one's work collapses. One starts becoming negative and pointing fingers, judging everybody, especially the Teacher, until one puts oneself

---

8   Major in the sense that their instinctive center attached special importance to it.

in the position that one has to leave the School.

Partial efforts, blind efforts and efforts in contradictory directions usually lead to a greater imbalance in the machine.

It is very difficult to find this School. One can be in the Fellowship of Friends for years without seeing it. If one finds it, it is very easy to lose it, and it is increasingly difficult to stay connected to it, as things never get easier. One gains nothing in terms of organic life; there is no recognition or degree. One does not become a better person or more intelligent. When one makes the right efforts, one simply becomes conscious of oneself and of one's environment, and yes, more balanced. If one misses the point, even by a degree, in the long run one ends up empty handed, vindictive and personal.

Nothing keeps one here, nothing but one's own efforts to become present, and one's connection to Higher Forces.

Expectations and infatuation with the form of the School or the Teacher are the sole responsibility of the individual and often prove to be tragic. To be precise, sometimes we attract people who think that believing literally and blindly in every word uttered by the Teacher (whether or not they heard it directly from him) is going to take them somewhere. Some also think that following his instructions as a slave or a sycophant will assure them redemption or spiritual gain of some kind.

Real man is not good or evil, real man is only conscious.
Gurdjieff

XVII

The first time I saw Robert Burton I did not even know it was him. A friend of mine, Jessica, had promised to introduce me to the Teacher that day at lunch time. We made an appointment at our restaurant, called at that time the Lincoln Lodge. I came on time and sat in the mezzanine waiting for her. There was an exercise then, when making an appointment, not to wait for a student for more than fifteen minutes. Well, I waited for more than half an hour and she did not show up. I asked around if anybody had seen her and was told that she was already in the building having lunch. I rushed to the table where she was quietly sitting with three other people, all male.

Totally identified, I told her how inconsiderate she was to have forgotten our appointment. She blushed and said "I'm sorry…" Before she finished her sentence I turned away and left, furious. Later she came to me and, after a few more apologies, she said, "That was him, you know." "That was who?" I said. "That was Robert I was sitting with. He asked me to join him for lunch and I was just talking to him about you when you rushed to the table. I told him you wished to meet him." I was quite surprised, truly incredulous, but Jessica just smiled and went on. "He said it was not written in your play to meet him there."

I met Robert Burton on Independence Day, at midday. Walter came to me and said he would introduce me to the man behind what I had then described to him as a "sacred atmosphere". There was a celebration in the front lawn of the main building of the property, now called the Galleria Apollo. Some people were playing Frisbee and others were sitting on the lawn under small trees. At the corner of the lawn there was a small group of students standing around a man and a woman who were sitting under a zelcova tree. The tree was so small at the time that one of the young men had to hold a white umbrella over the couple in order to shelter them from the scorching sun. As we approached them Walter said, "Hello Robert, this is Rolando. Rolando, this is Robert."

Robert swiftly got up and only just holding my hand he said, in a barely audible and kind voice, "Hello, Rolando. Maybe we can have dinner together sometime?" Almost immediately he sat down and turned back to talk to the lady. I briefly noticed the change of his tone as he addressed her. It became suddenly serious. I experienced the clear feeling that up until then I had been asleep. I had experienced higher states before; some induced by peyote, others by shocks, yet others achieved by long and sustained effort. But this time I had been put in a higher state by the sole presence of this man.

We then slowly walked away and, perplexed, I asked my friend, "Walter, who is this man?" He laughed softly and replied, "He is the Teacher."

I must say, he disarmed my every expectation of him, I felt his kindness, vulnerability, and humility as he touched my hand. He emerged from the molecular world to greet me, and brought me in for a few seconds. By the time he sat down, he had already turned away. He went on giving instructions to someone else, and I was left there, gleaming in wonder.

I said before, "I met Robert Burton…" I must rephrase it thus, "I met Presence within Robert Burton…" The man himself is just like a Nahua or a Maya Indian; he is that humble.

I promised myself then to move as soon as possible and live as near as possible to this man and work with him. I had verified for over a year the scope and quality of his influence. I had verified on my own the ideas that he and the rest of the School practiced. This man was in a state I had experienced before and did not know how to reach on regular basis. What struck me most is that he is in control of it.

He is present at will.

Soon after I received an invitation for dinner and was told to have my "burning questions" ready since Robert was seldom available. He had stopped teaching directly and one could have dinner with him only once a year. They told me that he was devoting his time to the construction and development of Apollo, which required a lot of traveling to the most civilized cities around the world in order to get ideas for the development of the estate. He also purchased art and impressions for our museum and encouraged young students to move to the heart of the School. As for the teaching, there were enough people in the inner circle capable of transmitting the ideas on a daily basis.

I did not have any "burning questions", and during dinner he asked me if I had been to Europe, and I replied that no, I had not. He then assured me I would go there soon. There were some visitors from Spain at the table, and noticing I was proficient in English, I was asked to translate during the whole dinner. At the end he told me I had to come back to dine with him again, since my role as a translator had prevented me from assimilating his teaching.

At dinner he spoke about Higher Forces, and of how when he started the School, he was hesitant to share this understanding with his students. But to his great surprise, most of them had experienced Higher Forces in their lives before meeting him.

The day after, while working in the vineyard, I mentioned Robert's comment on my visiting Europe to Walter; he gave me his usual kind and intelligent smile and said, "He means to take you with him in his next trip. But you have to be ready, for it will not be easy." When I asked him what that meant he replied, without changing his gentle mood, "You are young and handsome. He probably finds you attractive and wishes to take you as his boyfriend." Those last words, kind and plain as they were, hit me in the center of my organic being; they did not make sense at all. For one thing I never thought of myself as handsome, let alone thought of by another man as attractive, certainly not by this man. Walter said nothing more and the two of us went on working with the vines; a strained silence permeated our work.

I had already created the tendency to work with significant shocks like this one, and part of that work was to find out **what** within the machine had been shocked at the same time as separating from it. The character of the I's expressed internally and externally showed they were coming from the king of clubs, who was outraged by the perspective, and it expressed it with powerful strength.

"I was not going to go to Europe, thank you, I was not going to have a relationship with a man, thank you, I was going to pack my things and go back home, thank you very much." There was no sophistication in these I's, they only expressed the impulse to run away.

Of course I was not going to pack the same day and leave; I had to have some certainty about Walter's remarks. The next evening I went to dinner once again: every inch of me was tense. I had a stiff sense of awareness of everything and everybody at the table, especially of Robert. Yet while feeling the power of the instinctive force within me, I also noticed that I could be present to it. That was the first time I had the clear sensation of being trapped within the instinctive center, the back of my neck was hard as a rock. Robert was his usual clear, loving, and powerful Self that evening but I could not engage with him. I could not conceive that this man, whom I knew possessed the key to higher centers, would ask of me something like that. That evening, as he was saying good night, he kissed me on the forehead and said, "Relax, Dear." But he did not ask me to go to Europe with him, or to be his boyfriend or anything. Anyway from then on, every time I was invited to sit at his table or interact with him in any other way, the king of clubs appeared with the same force and fear.

I did not leave, I took this as another opportunity to study and separate.

Certainly Robert is a powerful being, and soon I realized that I can only reach him when I make the right efforts to achieve his silent power, which is nothing but the inconspicuous presence of higher centers. I had become acquainted with the quality of that state and the efforts necessary to attain it. Yet this shock put me face to face with a most powerful and intelligent opponent to the emergence of higher centers, the instinctive center.

Once the hydrogen of the shock had vanished, I worked with the residual I's that had an opinion about sex in general. The main line of action was to observe my own king of clubs' attitudes and habits regarding sex. It was very difficult to observe these most elusive parts of the machine, whose combination represents probably the major obstacle to awakening. On one hand I was dealing with the brain that keeps one connected to feminine dominance, the intelligence that rules every machine, the king of clubs. On the other hand I was trying to observe the sex center. I noticed I could not study this brain directly unless I was present, since its work uses up the very substance presence is made of.

As a by product of this experience, I noticed that my sex life was unconventional enough according to western standards. Judgment I's about anyone else's sex practices only revealed the unscrupulous nature of the instinctive center. That is, it prefers to focus on someone else's mechanics in order to cause one to stop making efforts to observe and control one's own. As for homosexuality, it is not part of my mechanics, and I have not verified this or any other mechanics can prevent higher centers from awakening. Additionally, the fact that a large number of people are neutral, if not positive, about homosexuality, proves that a negative attitude towards it is purely subjective. In general the king of clubs is totally against it, and the king of clubs controls the mass of humanity.

Ten years later I ventured into a relationship with Robert; at that time I was his photographer. I have had traumatizing experiences in my life, and this was not one of them. Curiously enough it was more difficult to work with the I's produced by the prospect, than to separate from the actual experience. I must say, it was not easy to find the right concentration in order to do something totally against the instinctive center, but it was not terribly bad: it was just very difficult. I laughed within myself afterwards thinking that, had I sorted this one before, I would have spared myself a lot of useless fear, negativity and imagination.

For one thing, I saw I was not going to be close to Robert on the level of functions. I had received shocks and omens indicating it. A few equivocal situations which created tension between us took place. One I remember happened once during one of those seemingly endless grape harvests. Several students were engaged in a friendly grape-cluster-battle, which were common during those long hours working under the blistering California sun. At the end of the day, Robert was walking down the terrace we were working on, when a student who was standing by me threw a cluster of red grapes at someone standing in front of Robert. This other student ducked and the cluster hit the Teacher right on his solar plexus, leaving a zinfandel stain on his white shirt. I saw the student who threw the grapes disappear under a vine, terror was in his eyes. I turned around and saw Robert approaching me, and pointing at the stain on his shirt he looked straight at me and said, "That was a good shot, Dear". "Thank you", I replied.

This was no act of heroism. It all happened so quickly: this student's terror, my not feeling guilty, Robert addressing me. However, Robert was not pleased a bit, and though he was not negative, he put a distance between us. This was one of several equivocal occurrences that put a damper on our relationship on that level. On a higher level I feel always united to him, even if as individuals we are completely different in many ways. I have learned to respond to his love, and I see him as a man in whom the divinity is active. I am grateful Higher Forces brought me to him and the inner circle.

Later on someone asked me if I had been seduced or lured into a relationship with him. I do not believe in seduction. That is just a term to hide a silent agreement between two parties (unless you are really credulous and easy to fleece, in which case even your dog knows he owns you). I took the experience as an experiment on doing what the machine refuses to do, observed my reactions, listened to other people's, and found out that people's reactions to this or any other event vary according to their mechanics and degree of consciousness. Some agree with the matter, some disagree with it, some are utterly upset by it, others instead, find it completely inconsequential, yet others just try to have a good time with it. In short, this and any other subject can be pondered from an infinite number of angles, all of which will seem right to an individual in the second state. Now, to be excessively against someone or something can lead to madness.

On the other hand, some people are lazy, both emotionally and intellectually. They are inclined to avoid any responsibility in their actions, and prefer to think they have been abused or seduced.

This is the Fourth Way, the way of the sly man, the way for people who know too much. Anyone who thinks he can get to Paradise, or whatever he calls it, by doing something he does not understand, is in the wrong place.

A good shock makes energy quickly.

Ouspensky

XVIII

I went back and forth from Mexico City to the heart of the School at least twice a year. I developed skills as a translator and learned a third language, which gave me more flexibility to travel. In fact we had been asked to travel around the world and support the developing centers. So at some point I did go to Europe, spent a few years in Italy and France, and visited several centers in Germany and the UK.

While living in Italy I saw Robert several times as he used to visit Europe on a regular basis. One time I was asked to go to the airport and collect a student who was to travel with him. I had met this student at Apollo, and we had worked together in the orchards. We had had many difficulties because of our cultural differences, but mainly because he was a real farmer and I was never going to become one. So he had to put up with someone he considered not only useless but a nuisance…

I was supposed to give him a small tour around downtown Milan and then accompany him to a restaurant where we would meet Robert. This student had never been to Europe. He arrived in Milan and was in a state of elation, which I somehow assimilated. When we finally met Robert he greeted me warmly, grabbed me by the arm and whispered in my ears, with a voice almost not his, "There is richness in you." I was about to say something when he suddenly turned his back on me and walked away with the students. His secretary at the time just waved at me, "Thank you. Good bye" and they left.

I was asked to pick up this student; I went out of my way in order to accommodate this request. Why had he excluded me? I stood there, all alone, staring at the Church of San Babila, with a burning sensation in my solar plexus, trying to stop every 'I' connected to the emotion. And I was lucky to engage in that effort for this was not the only time he would shock me that way in order to produce higher hydrogen within me. His words persistently returned to my field of awareness, "There is richness in you."

Friends are like the parts of a whole ... their whole consists of unity.

Dante

XIX

How, if Robert was not available on a regular basis, was I to receive his direct influence? I had decided not to be involved with him. It did not occur to me to become his friend, his favorite or anything like that. I felt connected to him and the School through Higher Forces and my efforts to be present. Well, I got lucky because, even tough externally we never seemed close then, I attracted octaves that involved working with him, without his or my choice.

(At this point it seems pertinent to mention that although the feeling of being in the Work never abandons me. It is only when I get exposed to Robert Burton's presence that I verify whether or not that is true. Now, there are times between encounters with him that my work is either feeble or sporadic. Then meeting him acts as an alarm clock; it is an unpleasant shock. On the level of the steward it creates the sense of urgency, but on the level of the machine things are much different.

When higher centers are asleep, the king of clubs becomes active and goes on to lead its existence undisturbed. It prevents the awakening of higher centers since this sheds life on the fact that its individual existence is of no real consequence to anyone. The instinctive center is therefore afraid of the emergence of higher centers as they tame its control over the machine. Robert Burton is the embodiment of higher centers. His appearance alarms the instinctive center, who not only is afraid of him but also dislikes him. The instinctive center, or lower self, makes every effort to distance itself from Robert, first through judgment, then through gossip, wit and slander. In some cases it gets really vicious. Once at a dinner someone stated this clearly. He said, "Robert, my lower self does not like you." Without losing his composure he replied, "Yes, mine does not like me either.")

Robert is a very creative teacher, and he is always looking for new ways to design opportunities for the three lines of work to take place. As soon as he espies a tendency or strength in one or more of his students, he does not hesitate to drive it to its highest possibilities. In this process one is given the opportunity to observe where one stands in relation to a given tendency or strength from the viewpoint of the Work.

Now, there was a time when a few younger students started to meet after work and on Sundays to play soccer in one of the lawns in front of the Galleria. In those days we had extra time after work and before the weekend concerts. Somebody bought a ball and started more or less to fool around with goals made out of sweaters and pots. I refused to participate in that activity because I had, in the past, played soccer with the aim to become a professional. Although it did not happen, I became very good and played in top teams all the way to college, so I was not interested in casual scrimmages. One day Robert saw his students playing on his front lawn, and to a certain extent enjoyed the view. He suggested that they start playing more formally. He bought them uniforms, shoes, professional balls and a couple of right sized goals, and asked them to play in a more organized way, but still without any discipline behind it.

It was not until he started to push them towards becoming a professional team that I found the octave interesting. We were to have a professional training, build up the required muscle and stamina in order to be able to enter the Northern California Soccer League. We needed a professional soccer field for that, and we had to build it ourselves, meaning the team members. All of this, the training, the clearing and development of the spot for the soccer field had to happen after work and on weekends, for it was not supposed to interfere with our assigned regular activities at Apollo. The creation of the team just added pressure to our already physically demanding lives. Plus most of the players were already in their late twenties. I myself was over thirty, which meant we were mostly past our prime for that sport.

Robert came often to see the team as we practiced and built the soccer field. He would give instructions to a few players, mainly those close to him as friends, invite them for dinner, and then drive away. During the development of the team he did not address me directly but twice. The first time was one afternoon when, after the whole team had leveled the spot for the soccer field, installed irrigation, conscientiously de-rocked and raked it by hand, I was given the task of driving a tractor with an iron net attached to it across the field, in order to make sure it was nice and smooth for seeding. It took nearly two hours to drive back and forth at a very slow speed. As I was about to finish the last round; I saw Robert's vehicle approaching. He waved at me to get off the tractor and come to him. I was surprised that he had come at that time of the day. It was about half past six in the middle of the summer. I thought he came to invite me for dinner or something. Well, he handed me a couple bottles of sparkling water and said, "You might need these." I thanked him and said I was almost finished. "Oh, by the way, Dear, I think my car made some marks on the field as I was following you. Could you please make sure to go back and erase them?" "No problem", I said. He drove away.

I walked around the field looking for the traces, and to my surprise I saw he had gone up and down, round in circles, left to right and across the field so many times, that he had destroyed my work. The field was a mess! I had to start all over from the beginning! I must admit that when I saw him leave without inviting me to dinner, the energy of negativity started to materialize. But when I saw what he had done, the extra work he had created for me at the end of the day, I smiled with respect for him, for he never hesitated to demand super efforts from his students. Apollo is the result of these demands.

My steward then became active and started to work on the energy Robert had unleashed. The feeling of being left out was relatively easy to work with, but then imagination would kick in. As I started to make efforts to remember myself, an "I" from the lower self said, "Not now, it is dangerous! You're driving a tractor!" It was so convincing because it came accompanied by a sense of fear.

I saw once again that the enemy within is indeed in control of the machine. For one thing, fear is not my chief feature, and I do not recall ever being afraid of driving a tractor. Later on I discovered that this same mechanical "I" came while driving a car trying to divide attention, and while sitting at a concert trying to divide attention. In short, this mechanical "I" always came as a reaction to the effort to divide attention, and it always said, "Not now." Even today, as I write and read these lines, the lower self is convinced that divided attention will prevent me from producing them properly. The lower self knows there is basically nothing within the sphere of human affairs that requires divided attention, so it sees it as an interruption. I believe this is the reason Gurdjieff said that the Work goes against Nature.

It was almost dark when I finally got off the tractor. I was in a clear state of awareness. Simultaneously the lower self started to think of this Teacher as a rascal and a trouble maker as much as I read Gurdjieff was. I also realized that students who loathe a teacher for being a trouble maker are not to blame; it is just that they lack the understanding to work with his demands, puzzles and tests. In that case, all they are left with is their essence and their lower self reacting to them.

"Good and evil live in perfect balance within every conscious teacher."

A few months later the field was done, the team was ready,

we entered the league, and at the end of the season we won the Northern California Championship. This Fourth Way teacher had taken a group of students who were just fooling around with a soccer ball on his front lawn and created a professional soccer team out of them, complete with a professional field, during their time off! It was far from easy and fun. I always thought that the team was an allegory of the School: We were all different players, used to different styles of game, often getting hysterical about each other, and lacking a unified style or tactics. For my part I found it extremely difficult to adapt to people who play European style; and never before had I played in the freezing rain with the fear of being struck by lightning!

Robert was not genuinely interested in soccer itself; being American, he did not even understand the rules. He never came to see us when we played in other cities. Whenever we played at home, he would come, sit and apparently watch the game. Yet he had a portable TV installed by his side, and would watch football or basketball instead, I never found out what. After the second season he had accomplished his aims, and withdrew from the octave. We stopped playing a few months later; mainly due to the number of the inevitable injuries. Today one can see llamas, horses and all kinds of livestock grazing in what once was a soccer field.

As for me, playing soccer came to an unexpected end. Ever since I was a child I chose to play the "left forward" position. I used to have the aim to score at every match at least once. When I did not succeed, the experience felt incomplete, even if my team won. Every time I scored a goal I would celebrate the typical way: screaming and running to the side of the field, performing a dance, or a series of jumps, etc. I did not know how important all this was for my machine until the day Robert asked me to stop such exaggerated expressions of excitement after scoring a goal. I was supposed not to make a big deal of it. He sent this message through several players.

My lower self's reaction was a big surprise for me. The first "I" was clear and straightforward. "He will have to find someone else to score goals for his team. I am not playing for him anymore." Naturally, I did not quit. But from then on I started to feel uneasy during games. I could not play wholeheartedly. My lower self became more and more hysterical. But I saw that Robert had pointed out a form of self-importance attached to my interest in soccer. I felt ashamed about this situation. Around that time I injured my right heel and decided to quit for good.

Later on someone suggested that perhaps Robert did not know how deeply identified with the event I was. It is all the same for the steward. I still had to start making efforts to separate as soon as I saw the lower self reacting to this particular shock.

It was said that, because this is the Fourth Way, friction and other opportunities for the Work have to be created by means of ordinary life events, and by taking advantage of students' mechanical inclinations. The soccer team is a good example of this. Similarly, through his students' skills and mechanical strengths, Robert has created a winery that produces world class wines, a premium olive oil that is amongst the ten best in the world, and an orchestra. In the process several students developed skills as musicians, cooks and architects, all on a high professional level. Of course these are just byproducts. The main purpose of it all has been to create opportunities for all the three lines of work to take place.

The value is not in the suffering but in the soul's desire.
                                            Catherine of Siena

XX

It is clear that Robert Burton saw the work of Higher Forces behind his resolution to start our School; and so did every student who has joined him in the effort to build and maintain this large scale endeavor. The fact that Robert and no one else was chosen as the leading force of such vast effort shows the maturity of his soul. The features of his physical body are favorable for the task. He has a natural disposition for leadership, and the ability to visualize large scale octaves and bring them to completion. He is also a charismatic man, able to motivate the most unlikely workers to join him in his endeavor, even if only temporarily. His charisma and physical beauty sometimes cause female students to fall in love with him as a man. Although he does not relate to that, there is no way he can prevent it. On the other hand, to fall in love with him, to be somehow infatuated or admire him as a man, is a typical sign of sleep and if one does not awaken to it, it remains an unhealthy condition.

He is a Teacher and his responsibility is, as he has stated, to create the right circumstances for higher centers to awaken. Most of the time he does this through very subtle and kind shocks, but sometimes he has to do it by straightforwardly shocking the lower self in order to generate a great amount of energy. In these cases, even when one successfully transforms the energy that he unleashes in one, the lower self remains wary of him. The shocks he provides are based on actual mechanics and real life circumstances; in the sense that they constitute reality for the lower self. So the lower self has it against him.

I saw him providing these shocks to his close students on a number of occasions, asking them to do things that seemed impossible or inconceivable. For example he often places as leaders of activities that require competence students who are incompetent or not as competent as those who have to follow their directions. I saw many people's work crumble in such situations. They were simply unwilling or unable to turn things into opportunities for the development of will. Yet those who work with these shocks become increasingly focused and sober and they feel lucky and grateful.

I can only provide personal examples of how he worked along these lines. Before I met Robert I heard that he said some of his students wanted to use him as their janitor. They would ask him questions to help them solve problems related to their organic existence. I avoided such kind of questions. But once, after having observed the tendency to get involved one relationship after another, I went and asked him if he thought relationships were good for my work. He paused for a moment, put his hand inside the pocket of his coat, as if he was trying to reach for his pen, and said: "You mean a relationship with me?" Feeling uncomfortable I replied, "No, that is not what I mean. I mean in general." Noticing my emotion he added, quite impersonally, "People waste a lot of energy in relationships." The answer was clear. Suddenly

I understood that when I asked this question I had not put the subject in the right perspective according to the Work. I was basically asking if it was alright to keep this mechanics and still work on myself. Although the question was awkward, he found a way to take advantage of that area of identification to create work for me.

From that moment on began a series of interactions with him that produced friction in the area of relationships. For example he would ask me to do things for him that required giving up or postponing a date; sometimes even in the middle of a date he would ask me to get up and go fetch my camera in order to take a picture for him. One time a lady sat on her own for a long time waiting for me; until she finally found someone else to drive her home; and that was the end of it. Other times he saw me talking to a lady and interrupted the conversation by calling her or me to his side. He was just toying with that identification but I knew that was his privilege. However, it was a constant challenge to keep calm.

I then saw that identification meant that my sense of identity was attached to a certain device and its mechanical manifestation.

Yet one day I met a lady whom I really liked and started spending time with her, doing all those things that one does when one likes somebody. Things seemed smooth and hunky dory for a while until one day we went to a concert at our Town Hall[9] and, as we entered the hallway we came face to face with Robert. I smiled at him. He looked straight into my eyes for a second and did not

9   Now called the "Prytaneion"

smile back but walked on to his seat. "Sometimes he is like that", I thought, and went on to listen to the concert, feeling quite uncomfortable.

The following day one of his secretaries at the time, who was also a very good friend of mine, came to me with a task from the Teacher. He said that I was to stop any connection with this lady because Robert's best friend was interested in her. So he wanted to save her for him. I jumped back, "I beg your pardon; how is he ever going to become a man if he cannot even compete for his partner?" My friend was very good, he just replied, "This is a School, Robert is the Teacher, and this is a task." Good enough, he could go now and leave me immersed in negativity. I had to act quickly on that, for I knew that when one cuts off the head of a negative "I" it becomes pure hydrogen. When one does not, it may drag one's will for days or months on end. I spent the whole afternoon trying to stop thoughts and getting used to the hydrogen.

I had gone through plays of suffering before, and I had worked with Rodney Collin's advice that having the right attitude in the face of suffering was essential for the creation of will. All I had to do was separate from the I's produced by the instinctive and sex center, and focus on whatever I had to do in the moment. Every time they reappeared, I was to cut their heads and use the hydrogen.

It took me considerably less time to transform the energy of the shock than the first time I received one of that nature. But still I went through quite a few sleepless nights. I used to get up at dawn and go jogging, just to get rid of energy I could not transform. This time I was not working in the dark. I was aware of the instinctive center, and what is more, I started to see the difference between the deputy steward and the steward. The deputy steward focuses on observing; the steward, instead, has to act upon what it sees. Mainly I was engaged in doing what the machine does not want to do.

After a while I did manage to let go of the matter; what I had gained internally was far more important than what I had to lose externally. It was not until then that I went to Robert and thanked him for having provided me with this opportunity. He gave me an unexpected answer as usual. "See Dear, for you it is mechanical. You will find another girlfriend by the end of the summer. He does not have the time to court this one because he has to travel and support his Teacher." I was sober enough by then to agree with this. In fact Robert had told me before that his relationship with this student was special; for the student was primarily an emotional support for him, and I respected that. Robert never told me directly why he was creating this or that situation. He simply did it and it was up to me to find out, through self remembering and self observation, what I was supposed to control or develop. He successfully used the machine's tendency to pursue relationships in order to generate a great amount of energy. Later on I verified that I did waste energy in this area; and I figured I needed to find the right circumstance that would help me neutralize this form of waste; but I did not have a clue about how to create it by myself; my only hope was in a task or a play coming from a higher source.

As Robert suggested, by the end of the summer I had attracted a new relationship. Luckily this was the play that would change not only my attitude toward the subject, but also toward the way I saw myself in the Work. Without going into details, all I can say is that it was a play of madness, in all directions, which allowed me to see that at the base of these mechanics, was the machine's imaginary picture; and at the base of imaginary picture there was a misunderstanding. That is, confusing sex energy with emotional energy. I believe that what Orage describes as "emotional love" is based on this delusion[10]. I did really hit the bottom, and when this play was over, my work became more constant.

Human affairs are really of no importance, but the lower self attaches importance to them in order to prevent one from pursuing the awakening of higher centers. After all, this life is all the lower self has. Time proves that the pursuits of the lower self are nothing more than temporary whims. For some people these pursuits are related to sex, for others to money, food, or comfort.

---

10   Orage's book "On Love"

The tasks offered to you have the aim to help you. If you hesitate or refuse them, you refuse help.

Ouspensky

XXI

Soon after the soccer octave was over, Robert embarked on a series of fundraising dinners and events to develop and embellish Apollo. Such fundraisers, which go on to this day, have put the School under a great amount of pressure, both financial and physical. Over the years, these fundraisers have caused a number of students to get exasperated and cease to understand the School (even though they knew that part of the Work entails the exasperation of the lower self).

Every time Robert requests or suggests something with the aim to keep the three lines of work alive, the lower self consents to it in the hope that by doing so it might dig up some kind of personal benefit, spiritual progress or status. After a while, noticing there is no personal gain in the creation and maintenance of the School, the lower self loses interest and starts to resist or evade the Teacher's requests and suggestions in this area. When one does not have a steward or one's Self to respond to Robert's aim to keep the Work and the School alive, one's lower self inevitably drags one out of his influence. One then starts to disagree, oppose, judge, and become increasingly resentful towards him.

Anyway, during these fund raisers Robert asked one of his friends (who was a photographer) to start taking pictures at the events and mail them to the guests. There were other professional photographers available but he chose this one student for the role. It happened that this student started to get a bit weary of the job, since it was fairly repetitious, demanding and tiring. Without asking Robert, he just started to have me substitute for him, first sporadically, later more frequently (at that time I had developed some skills as a photographer). Robert did not seem very happy with this, since every time I showed up boxed in a tuxedo with my camera ready he would just ask me straight on, "Where is Freddy?" I would reply that I did not know where Freddy was. Without adding anything he would just walk away and ignore me for the rest of the evening. This short conversation went on for a while. Once he started getting used to this situation, he asked me if I could show him a few pictures I had taken of him during events, and I did. He liked them and asked for copies to share with his friends.

From then on he started to ask me for photos of the most varied and unusual subjects: flowers blooming in the fields, a tiny nest sitting at the very top of a tree, a new piece just purchased for the Galleria collection, a student sitting by the piano looking out the window... Once I had to get on an aircraft and take aerial pictures of a fire that devastated part of the land near our property. These requests came at the most untimely moments such as, when I was having lunch, or getting ready for a concert or a date, and I had to act immediately. On one occasion I was in the shower and the friend I was living with at the time told me that the Teacher was on the phone and wished to speak to me. I said I was in the shower and

I would call back. Next thing I see is my friend's hand reach into the shower, turn the water off and put the phone on my ear. I heard Robert's voice saying, "Dear, there is a rooster we just purchased in the Galleria kitchen; do you mind taking a picture?" "When do you wish this done?" I asked, dripping. He replied, "Oh, please finish your shower Dear. Thank you."

I took so many pictures of things and people, and I never knew what he did with them. Sometimes he asked me to give them to other students. Other times he told me to give them to him, and when I did, he acted like he had "forgotten" about the matter. I went through this process of going out of my way and taking pictures simply because he asked me to, and also because it made me feel good about myself. Then I began to get tired of it, and to resent the consequences of having to leave in the middle of work, or missing an appointment, or a date, just to take a picture. I always responded promptly to his requests, yet at some point the negative emotion of resentment started to sink in. I never knew when he was going to call, for he could call any moment. Even when he was traveling in Europe he would call and ask me to take a picture and send it overnight. This extra work was on top of my regular gardening job and the already time consuming photography octave itself, which required developing, sorting out and mailing, during my spare time.[11]

In the beginning I was always willing to take pictures for him, I was even happy to do it; it was mechanical. But he asked for so many pictures, so often and at the most inconvenient moments that I ended up exasperated,

11   At that time digital photography was not available.

unable to do it unless I saw it as an act of will.

Around that time he asked me to meet him at the Gallery one afternoon just before sunset, bring my camera and make sure to load black and white film in it. I arrived early and sat on one of the sofas facing west, waiting for him. The main salon in the Gallery has two French doors facing west which lead to a formal rose garden; their frames create a cross, Christian type. Robert arrived as the sun was going down and sat by me in silence... As time went by my instinctive center became alert. He then told me to be ready because when the sun came down, it cast the shadow of a Greek column supporting a trellis outside the doors, aligned exactly with the cross. He wanted a picture of that. He said it was an omen. I calculated it would be about ten minutes before that happened, so I had time to relax and be present. Just then he said: "Our School is greater than that of Christ's." Quite unexpectedly I observed irritation when I heard these words, and became tense. I felt the impulse to smile and say something in agreement but did not know what. We remained silent for what seemed an eternity. A chain of thoughts set off in my brain in relation to what he had just said. I felt compelled to give that subject attention, but refrained. I just used the energy of the shock. I kept struggling to stop thoughts when all of a sudden Robert held my hand and added, "Christ is helping us awaken." The lower self became more and more irritated, and I had to renew the effort to let go of the "I's". "...Yes", I said.

We sat in silence for a long time until the shadow of the Ionic column was cast upon the cross. I suddenly became present as this was happening and saw a clear symbol of our School at the time. The irritation was there but I was present. Then I heard Robert say, "You can take a picture now, Dear". He got up and left the room. As soon as he left, my lower self became agitated and produced the impending impulse to leave, but I made the aim to keep the state and wait until the symbol vanished.

When I got home I realized the instinctive center became negative as soon as Robert left the room. This time I noticed that the lower self indeed is afraid of the awakening of higher centers. I clearly felt it wanted to pull me down as soon as possible. It became impatient and hysterical and tried to make me interested in all kinds of "important" things to do: read a book, have rampant sex, or start an argument.

I framed a copy of that picture and used it for a while as a reminder of that moment; I do not know what Robert did with the copy I gave him. Later on I tried to figure out what had caused negativity in the lower self. The key was in one of the first "I's" that manifested as Robert spoke to me. It went something like, "Why is he telling me that? I do not need to be persuaded." Certainly vanity is one of the chief manifestations of the lower self, but the most surprising discovery is that it takes credit and furthermore, it puts its identity in knowledge that is none of its concern. Whether or not we are a School on the scale of that of Christ's has nothing to do with the lower self. Nevertheless it has an opinion and an attitude towards that statement. Whether or not Christ is helping us awaken has to do with higher centers. So why does the lower self take the matter personally? It just shows its unscrupulous nature. It can use anything to start an argument in order to keep higher centers asleep, even information that is unimportant to its existence.

In a higher state, I know we are a School and I know I was looking forward to working with a man like Robert Burton.

Of course I have hit intervals in my relationship with this extraordinary man; especially when I was his photographer. For many months, before he got used to me, he simply ignored me during events. I worked steadily on inner considering, and when I did not, I resented him. I will share one episode that helped me bridge a major interval in my relationship with him. It happened during the time I was reading a passage in Ouspensky in which he describes the attributes of a conscious being; and started to look for those attributes in Robert, rather inquisitively.

I was particularly interested in verifying whether or not he had any power of telepathy; and if so, what he made with it. For a few weeks this question was in my mind as I took pictures of him during events. I wondered how it could be possible to verify this since Robert was not speaking one word to me at the time; plus I myself had no telepathic powers or anything like that. All I would do was to look at him intently, sort of challenging him, as I took pictures of him. I felt ridiculous when I realized that nothing happened. This went on for some time during which I just dreaded working for him.

Finally, one evening, I focused my camera on him as he was raising his glass to give a toast before dinner. (Usually this was the last picture I took at formal dinners. Afterwards I would leave the room). This time he paused for a moment, looked at his glass and instead of giving a toast, he said, "Why do I have to read your mind if I have Shakespeare?" He put his glass down and had his first bite. He briefly looked in my direction, above my head. I understood I could now leave the room.

Payment, in the true sense of the word, must be useful not only to you, but to someone else- to the school.
Ouspensky

XXII

Once Robert was asked if he knew who the richest student in the Fellowship was. He replied that he did not know and added, "But if they join the inner circle, Higher Forces will start using their money". Our never-ending fundraisers have shed light on this issue. They are expensive, and for a long time they were extremely expensive. Robert would become available again on a regular basis, but only those who paid could join him and learn how to be present directly from him.

Whether one pays or works for them, attending fundraisers is only a small part of the deal. Robert often says, "You have to show up twice at these events." When one pays or works for an event, one has only found a way to bring one's physical body to the experience. Yet in order to really profit from it, one has to succeed in awakening one's astral body through the experience; the event itself is just a favorable circumstance.

Guests are asked to arrive one hour prior to an event; this allows them to make the effort to control whatever groups of I's are taking space before the Teacher actually enters the room. What is more, in order to help students find the right concentration to work, a short live concert and a poetry reading take place before the actual teaching event.

When Robert teaches, he addresses higher centers. He often shocks lower centers in order to release the energy necessary for higher centers to appear, yet the effort to awaken higher centers remains one's task. In other words, Robert teaches outside of time; one who wishes to learn from him must bring oneself outside of time. When one remains in lower centers, one often ends up puzzled or negative.

With the money raised at these events we built a world class rose garden. We purchased antique fountains and statues. We built streets lined with palm trees, rose trees and orange trees, a restaurant, a beautiful park complete with hundred year old olive trees and palm trees. We built a Greek amphitheater and once a year we invite some of the best ballet dancers in the world to perform for us. Our museum collection increased significantly. In short, we created a very refined environment for our meetings and events, all from our own pockets and physical efforts.

The fundraising events were just part of these efforts; crews had to be organized for the design and construction of all the venues. Sometimes we had professional skills involved, yet a few of us were required to learn the profession in the field, so to speak. Some of us became improvised masons, carpenters or gardeners (like in my case). Yet others discovered that their essence was more at ease with the job demanded from them than the career they had originally chosen in life. We worked under pressure since everything that was poured into the development of the property came from us.

In Touch With The Miraculous

Robert keeps everyone working under tremendous pressure. He aims high with every fundraiser, and the inner circle somehow manages to make it work every time. We are only just finishing building one venue, and new fundraisers are already starting for the next one. As for the construction crew, he always sets short term deadlines. He encourages students to produce a garden or a piazza within a few weeks or so. Once we are about to meet the deadline, he increases the pressure by adding more details to the construction, or changing the design in a way that requires destroying and rebuilding within a few days, more than often working long hours or into the night.

And how did we get all of these old palm trees, some of them more than a hundred years of age? Robert gave the task to a student, who over the years proved to be an articulate and able dealer, to scan the surrounding cities, square by square, in search for mature palm trees to buy or trade for. He would negotiate with home and nursery owners for the purchase or trade of their old palm trees, and he was very successful. Then the landscape crew would drive to a different town, dig out the palm, and transport it back to Apollo. Later on we would go back to recreate their landscape: laying a new lawn, planting trees and flowers, etc… all on a high level.

When one is in the inner circle one understands why one makes efforts to support the Work as staged by Robert Burton. One is aware of the need to keep the Work alive, the structure of the Work being Robert's duty. One understands that the School exists within one. When one is in the outer circle one sees oneself as separate from the School. That is, one sees an institution comprised of people and their teacher, and one expects that in exchange for one's donations to the institution one will get something tangible for oneself.

As one falls asleep, one moves towards the outer circle.

I should probably be able to find the funds necessary for (Gurdjieff) to place his work on a proper footing, and also bring him more prepared people. But of course I still had a very vague idea in what this work might consist.

Ouspensky

XXIII

Looking back in time I now realize that Robert Burton has been able to keep a privileged number of students working together in the same direction for a period of almost forty years. He has accomplished this by creating long term, large scale second and third line octaves. By means of these octaves students have learned to keep their focus and work together as friends, or at least to interact with each other in a friendly way. Although the choice of these privileged people is in the hands of Higher Forces, each individual must have the intrinsic desire to remain connected to this vast effort. Over the years a number of people have contributed financially, others by offering their time and skills or both; but the denominator in this limited number of students is the agreement that one's work requires constant help from others with the same aim and understanding.

In the Fourth Way a man cannot work all by himself.

Thus a 365 acre vineyard was created, a winery built to suit, world class gardens and streets, man-made lakes, buildings for the performing arts, restaurants, and a private school; all of which took many years to develop, but also need constant maintenance. Students were encouraged to purchase land and build homes in the little town of Oregon House, where the heart of the School is established. A small community developed around the property purchased by the School.

A network of men number four in the pursuit of a common aim was encouraged by the Teacher.

As said before, Robert often places as leaders of activities that require competence students who are incompetent or not as competent as those who have to follow their directions. This happens even today, and it is an intentional way to create friction, energy and work; when one is lucky one gets to play roles on both sides of the coin.

Once I played a leading role in an octave where I was rather ignorant. My essence was really troubled by the experience, since I was asked to lead one of the several farming octaves. While not a farmer in essence, I tried to be one in personality. Despite the fact that I could not think in terms of the octave itself, I still saw myself being bossy and sometimes arrogant, pretending I knew what I was doing. Plus the lower self experienced a certain pleasure in having people under its command.

Fortunately that experience lasted only a short time. It ended when an actual farmer moved into the octave and started to do things according to nature's rhythms instead of his own notions. This student really had a hard time with my mechanics, simply because he understood what had to be done in the moment, in terms of farming, and he saw my mechanics as pure denying force in the triad. He put it plainly one day by saying that I did not need to turn farming into an emotional situation; "Farming is about doing, being on time, moving steadily; not about showing up when you feel like it, telling stories, taking pictures, and making friends."

On another occasion I was assigned the octave of translating Robert's book, Self Remembering into Spanish, which indeed was part of my expertise. I was to distribute chapters amongst Spanish speaking students, edit them and produce a final edition. Robert appointed a student to work with me. She was supposed to review my texts and correct them if necessary. That student was famous for speaking five languages, all poorly, including her own. Needless to say the whole matter became a comical wrestle. She did not know enough grammar to correct the text but still would want me to make corrections. She could never explain what was wrong and how it was supposed to be corrected. All she could say was, "It does not sound good; make it sound good." I worked with this situation for a while but sent the message to Robert that I needed someone with at least some proficiency in the use of their own language.

My request was heard and promptly acted upon. Yet, if things were bad for the lower self, they just got worse when a student newly arrived from Spain was assigned to review the final text. She had pursued similar studies to mine but in Spain. She knew her Spanish perfectly. The problem was that her Spanish and my Spanish were very different indeed. So we sat together and, as we started to read through the lines, she decided that the Spanish was too Mexican. Every paragraph had to be rephrased according to the "true Spanish" from Spain.

On a personal level I really enjoyed working with her. It was like playing tennis with a hard to beat opponent. However, the octave became a never ending quarrel. She brought her dictionaries; I brought mine. And we would sit for hours, unable to get through a page in agreement. When Robert learned about this he made his final move. An English speaking student who knew some Spanish was appointed to sit between us, with a coin in his hand, and every time the least sign of an argument started, he would just flip it and that was it. Tails was Spain, heads was Mexico. This solution, unacceptable as it was for both sides, had to be accepted. Naturally the text suffered considerably in the process. Eventually she stopped working and moved back to Spain, never to be seen again.

For my part things did not finish there. A few more students were thrown into the already boiling pot; one from Argentina who did not speak English at all, and one from Guatemala who was bilingual and spoke Spanish diluted with English. Things got worst when the already completely-lacking-in-style text was sent to a publisher in Argentina and there it got modified once more in order to fit Argentinean Spanish. When I received a copy of the document I hardly recognized it. Other translation teams did not have this problem since their language is one and the same; while in Spanish there are some twenty versions, all correct. I then realized that I had to give up my identification with the use of Spanish,

In Touch With The Miraculous

otherwise I was definitely giving up my inner work. For there I was, working on the translation of a book about Self Remembering in the deepest state of identification. Although Robert was active in this matter, he never told me anything about it, he was aware of its irrelevance. He just kept sending whoever.

I envision Robert as a generator of energy, or higher hydrogen if you will. He uses many different tools to generate this energy within his students. But the lower self finds this hydrogen unbearable and wishes to get rid of it as soon as it feels it is circulating. Moreover, when the lower self concludes that Robert teases and tricks it all the time, it starts to resent him. Robert does not care about this. He knows that a student who has his steward in place is going to take advantage of every opportunity he provides.

According to what I read from people who actually knew Gurdjieff, sometimes he used more direct and blunt techniques. He sometimes made fun of his students, or yelled at them, or made them dig trenches and then fill them up again. Robert is more subtle in that sense; he does not yell at us or ask us to dig trenches, but rather to help him build Apollo beautiful. As he helps us awaken, over the years he has created a wonderful environment to be present to.

Fragments Of An Enduring Teaching

Here we can only direct and create conditions, but not help.

Gurdjieff

XXIV

While taking photographs for events at Apollo I had to work with three kinds of settings: there were the formal dinners with a dress code of tuxedos and long gowns. Then there were less formal receptions and teaching dinners both with a dress code of coat and tie for men, and dress for ladies. I had developed a technique to take a picture when people were not looking or posing, for I do not appreciate posing pictures. So I used a wide range lens in order to be able to shoot from a distance without being noticed, and zoom in to get a portrait. Most photographers observe that the moment people become aware of the camera, their body language and gestures change. At this moment I would withdraw without shooting; then I would search for a better moment. Working with formal dinners and teaching dinners was relatively easy. People were mostly in kings of centers and the pictures usually turned out well. The only difficulty was that since the king of clubs was active, sometimes people came out rather stiff, especially when Robert was nearby. I already mentioned that, in general, one's king of clubs becomes very active when the Teacher is near. It tries to look busy.

I had the aim to take pictures of students when they were in true personality or in essence, for sometimes they were obviously in false personality. But this is the way it is meant to be, since the Work is intermittent. My role as a photographer allowed me to zoom into this particular state of affairs. One moment I saw someone in essence, the next moment the quality of their presence had changed; it became affected. On the other hand, something similar happened to me. I had the aim to portray the best in people, and worked toward it, waiting for the moment when something of a finer nature would appear in their presence. Yet often I found my lower self judging what I saw through the lens and ignoring the person for the rest of the evening.

Receptions were a more difficult arena, since everybody was scattered around the gardens or the different rooms in the Galleria where they took place, mostly left to their own devices. Robert used to sit surrounded by his close friends and he would occasionally call a student over to him to exchange some words; but everybody was pretty much on their own, with friends of their choice. Food was served informally and wine was served copiously. In short, an atmosphere was created that made it very difficult to keep one's focus in the Work. Within this particular environment one could easily notice all kinds of interactions amongst students that were unrelated to the Work. Robert would sit there watching in silence. Then he would call someone to talk with them and sometimes give them a task or a personal exercise.

Seen from the second state of consciousness, these gatherings hardly made us look like an esoteric school. At best we looked like a glamorous social tribe, where all kinds of emotional and sex energy were generated and exchanged. But the Teacher was, as usual, well at work during them. I once asked him why we had these informal gatherings, since they did not help the development of kings of centers, like formal dinners and meetings did. "Yes", he said, "Formal events help you develop kings of centers. Receptions are about **you**. They are about what **you** are."

After he answered this question he became active in relation to what I was doing at the reception. Every time I engaged in conversation with someone, he would call the person to his side, talk to them and then send them to get someone else. He did this a number of times in a row, and every time I would remain alone in the middle of the gathering, until someone else came. I started a conversation, and almost immediately Robert would call that person to his side. I started to feel irritated and, as I was about to go on taking pictures, he called me by his side and said: "Can you see the hand of that god in the corner? Can you please take a picture for me?" I turned my head and saw, above the crowd of students, the hand of Mercury[12] outstretched, pointing upwards. I smiled as I took the picture, and then turned around to thank him, but he was gone.

Every time Robert got up and left a reception, the volume of conversation increased. It was then time to go home.

It was at these receptions that I discovered some undermining tendencies that otherwise would have remained in the darkness of the second state. The most insidious of them was the very pleasant tendency to spend

---
12   That sculpture has been gilded and sits now on top of a column in the middle of a roundabout.

In Touch With The Miraculous

my social life on the level of the seven of hearts, forgetful of the need to make effort. This level of attention kept me witty and fun, especially with the ladies, and made my evening a sort of obladi-blada experience.

A student told me that Robert requested that I stop interacting with the guests and focus on my job as a photographer. This was, in the beginning, very difficult to agree with, because my center of gravity feeds on people and conversation. However, it was providential in terms of the Work, for I was asked to focus on my job. This required me to observe and photograph the best in everybody without interacting with them, and to keep Higher Forces in mind.

A believer who has not had the experience of what is discussed herein cannot pass judgment on the secret things of God.

Miguel de Molinos

XXV

Have I ever doubted that this is a School?

When one is in the struggle to become present, one is working at the level of attention of the steward: one is in kings of centers. It was already mentioned that when one sustains **this** level of attention, the king of clubs becomes active. This is where doubt enters as a whisper, as a distraction introduced by the lower self. Doubt exists on the level of lower functions. One who has not experienced a higher state, or who has forgotten about it, is prone to listen to the voice of doubt.

Also, one who is negligent in the Work is subject to doubt.

The focus of the struggle is in the achievement of **that** which one already knows and wishes for; that is, the memory and taste of presence. In a higher state of consciousness all doubt disappears; one is the very thing one is looking for. Additionally, one recognizes those who are in a higher state, and those who are not.

I remember one morning at a formal breakfast I was struggling to be present throughout the event. My work was mainly to stop imagination and unnecessary talking. When we sat at the table, I knew I was succeeding in keeping a quiet mind. There came a moment when I had the distinct sense of getting through the invisible curtain of sleep. I looked around the table when I heard Robert say, "You see? Your higher centers are awake now. And your nine of hearts is active too." He was looking directly at me across the table. I noticed a burning sensation in my solar plexus and felt my lower self becoming alarmed and frightened. "The nine of hearts is promoting presence," Robert said, fixing his happy eyes on me. I noticed again, as every time I see his true being, that not only is he always present, but also that he is a radiant, powerful being. I looked at a student sitting nearby him. He was looking at his plate and was fast asleep. Robert grabbed my sight again and said, "You are awake, you see."

The lower self felt embarrassed, afraid and hysterical. I looked around the table. There were some fifty students at the breakfast. I noticed that some of them were quiet and neutral, others were not there.

That happened around the time when we started to practice the Sequence. Prior to this event I had made consistent efforts to stay out of imagination by means of this new tool we had been given.[13] I had not gone through any particular type of stress or suffering; I was simply trying over and over to stay out of imagination as I intoned the Sequence. I felt grateful that I met Robert and other students at the end of such efforts. I had the clear understanding that Robert is always in the present,

---

13   A Sequence of efforts intended to promote and sustain Presence.

waiting for us to join him, inviting us and creating the right circumstances for us to succeed. Indeed, when we are present we keep him company.

But waves of imagination are like the heads of the hydra, once you cut one off, two more grow right away. Thus, the Work is never-ending. When the breakfast came to an end Robert said, "Try not to lose this state. Stay where you are as long as possible, my Dears." I walked away from that breakfast still in a higher state. There are no words to describe what it was like to walk into the rose garden then. Many "I's" were nervously crowding around my presence; yet I was sober and strong.

Doubt is in the second state, and we try to move away from that. We strive for the third state; we strive for certainty.

In Touch With The Miraculous

Influence C appears to refer to the actual work of a higher man upon his intimate students.
R Collin

XXVI

During the time Robert spent in privacy the Fellowship of Friends grew and developed around the world, in some cases without his knowledge or direct influence. When he became more and more accessible to all, he began hosting a series of meetings and formal teaching events that attracted large numbers of students, many of whom did not know him personally and had never interacted with him. Some of these students were even prominent teacher-figures in the outer circle, and held roles of prestige amongst younger students.

It has been said before that when Robert teaches, he speaks to higher centers, and has to use techniques to bypass lower centers. The form of his teaching is somewhere between Mayan hieroglyphs and Beelzebub's Tales to his Grandson, sprinkled with whatever else may help to illustrate it. Students who were not used to this began to get confused, then alarmed, and eventually outraged by it. I described some aspects of this teaching in a separate document.[14]

That was a most interesting moment in the history of our School, for the Fellowship of Friends lost a few hundred people. All kinds of students with all kinds of roles walked away in search of a different teaching that made sense to them. Robert did not make sense anymore. When

14   A Further Effort

the outer circle met a conscious Teacher for real, they got totally confused and left. But the School remained almost intact, for we hardly lost a focused student.

In the end Higher Forces chose who to keep and who to release. Students in our School consistently are about 1,800; those who have left are about 10,000.

In Touch With The Miraculous

Your eyes look earthward, mine look up.
Cristina Rossetti

XXVII

We observe other people's mechanics from the point of view of what we call in the Work a "play of features", but the focus is on observation and control of our own as we try to be present. When we withdraw our attention from other people's mechanics and take the time to direct it toward our own, we observe that a feature in us reacts to a feature in them. We have to apply this tool when interacting with the Teacher, since we react mechanically to his influence and presence. At the same time we need to keep in mind that a conscious being acts intentionally through his features in essence. He uses them as tools for teaching and enhancing our possibilities to be present.

When one criticizes the Teacher's actions and methods, one is projecting a personal weakness in him, and what is more, one is asleep. Ouspensky's idea of mirrors applies here. As we divide our attention, we see that the lower self projects its weakness in others, including the Teacher. I discovered this a while ago, when I started paying attention to judgment I's about the Teacher. I realized that the lower self judged him in areas of sleep I was unaware of in myself. Additionally, I would hear other student's judgment I's about the Teacher's eating habits, or the way he spends money, or his sexual life, etc. I observed that in every case the area a person criticizes constitutes a blind spot they have not thought about or dealt with in themselves. In other cases people would judge the Teacher from an attitude or prejudice acquired through education within their social environment.

I did have judgment I's towards him in some areas and I worked with them as I observed them throughout the years. But there were a few subjects of judgment which were particularly difficult for me to work with; of these I will give one example.

A while ago Robert requested that some students scanned all kinds of texts and art which we thought contained the hidden message of using the physical body to promote the state of Divine Presence. As we embarked on this study, we came across many schools, traditions, and individuals who actually engaged in the same, if not a similar effort to our own. I was assigned the area of Mesoamerica and spent several years studying various texts and views on the subject. I became proficient in the available literature.

Robert asked me to send him a text on the subject, and I wrote a seventy two page document. It came back right away with the request to make it simpler and shorter. After a few days I reduced it to eighteen pages. "Shorter, please," was his response. I finally produced a two page introductory document to Mesoamerica and a couple of pages with quotations illustrating the work of esoteric schools before the Spanish invasion. Initially (meaning the first three years) he had a hard time relating to the material as it is expressed in a language completely foreign to the Western mind. Nothing happened for four years. In the meantime I kept reading and absorbing the information.

In Touch With The Miraculous

After a while I started to have a clear idea of esoteric schools and culture in that part of the world. As I became more acquainted with it, the lower self started to take it personally, mainly because of my Nahua[15] origin. I did not notice it directly but started to observe judgment as Robert used the material for his events. I noticed that, from my viewpoint, he would misinterpret the material, misquote sources, and intentionally mispronounce names. My lower self grew tense at an event as it unfolded; but most of the time I managed to act from the steward –by then we had developed a series of one syllable work I's that allowed us to refocus on Presence at once.

The day after an event I would send him notes explaining, first indirectly, and later on quite directly, how he had to present certain ideas in order not to give the impression of being an ignorant in the subject, but it was of no avail. The following event he would just say exactly what I had told him not to say, in exactly the way he wanted. I could feel my head swelling with fire every time he said something I disagreed with. Once in a while he would ask me questions at events which were either absurd or unrelated to the subject. I would provide tense, monosyllabic answers.

As time went by he asked me to research other subjects and individuals' work. My task was to let him know whether I thought they carried an esoteric message he was trying to convey at a given moment. According to my understanding, some of them were clearly engaged in the development of consciousness, others instead, were not. I sent my findings to Robert. Yet he would use whatever

15   One of the main nations within the Mesoamerican world

Fragments Of An Enduring Teaching

and whoever he wished, whether or not I had told him their work had any connection with esoteric schools or ideas. I started to observe an increase of judgment and impatience as I attended events, to the point that I considered seriously to stop helping him in this area –of course I did not. Sometimes I felt clearly that he was teasing my lower self by doing all this.

It seemed to me that, the more he noticed I was identified with my opinions, the more he toyed with the information I had given him. I knew he did that in general to other students, but when he did it in the areas I had studied it really irritated my lower self.

The lower self attaches importance to what it thinks it knows.

I started to deal with this circumstance as we do when we encounter a negative emotion: I took it as hydrogen to transform in the moment. Every time I would hear him say something I strongly disagreed with, I would just say "Drop", and use the hydrogen to be present. As I succeeded and became present I saw how he uses information from esoteric and exoteric sources and disarranges it in a kaleidoscopic way, always conveying this same simple message: "Try to be present now; try this new method."

It does not really matter who said what; what matters is the simple message Robert is trying to convey: "Try to be present now."

In order to understand a conscious teacher, one must

become familiar with the way he teaches, but more importantly, one has to try to be present as one is exposed to his teaching. Also, when one is in a higher state, all of one's I's related to whatever the lower self thinks it knows are seen as pure illusion.

Judgment is a veil. When one judges the world, one fails to see it as it is. But when one judges a conscious being, not only does one fail to see him, but one misses one's chance to become what he is.

Should one of us remember and one of us forget, I promise you what I will do... I am content to wait for you.
                              Cristina Rossetti

Notes on a trip with Robert

I mentioned before that the feeling of being in the Work never abandons me. Yet it is only when I get exposed to Robert's presence that I verify to what extent I have been engaged in the right effort. Thus one of the advantages of going to events is to be able to measure the result of my efforts. Now to travel with him means to be exposed to his presence on a daily basis. That is a remarkable situation, because Robert is a being who dwells in the present.

I have dealt with him on a fairly regular basis over the years, and I have met him several times during his trips by chance; however, I did not travel with him as part of his supportive students. He has invited me to join him several times in the past -consistently on a short notice- but I had to decline because of my life commitments. Once I told him we needed to arrange our trip in advance and he gave us a date. We made the necessary arrangements and just a few days before we were supposed to depart, he changed the date again; so nothing happened.

The prospect of traveling with him on these terms was an opportunity out of the ordinary. Yet the lower self was always alarmed and felt lucky that I had to decline invitations- mainly because it is afraid of flying and gets claustrophobic in hotel rooms. Also it does not consider the Teacher as its friend.

In Touch With The Miraculous

Finally a gap came in my schedule and I was able to accept his invitation to travel to Mexico for a week. This time additional fear sprung from a deadly virus which had spread in Mexico City. Nevertheless in this occasion I worked with that, for there was nothing impending that prevented me from accepting the invitation. I was to meet Robert and four students in Mexico City a day after their arrival.

I flew in late the night after they had arrived and was further delayed by a closed access to the city. When I finally got to the hotel room, I found a message saying that I had to contact them in the morning. When I called, his secretary told me to go to the hotel restaurant shortly before nine, reserve a table for six and wait for them. So I did.

Robert arrived and gently greeted me with a kiss on the forehead. I noticed the lower self felt uncomfortable to be kissed by him in public. The pull of Mexican feminine dominance was so strong. "Men do not kiss men in a macho society". Anyway I dismissed the "I" and was happy to see him. He quietly sat down and asked, "What time did you get here, dear?" "Past midnight", I replied, and added, "The main access to the city was closed for repair so we had an extra hour delay." Without looking at me he pointed upward and made himself comfortable in the chair. We remained silent for a long time; in fact that was pretty much the tenor of our time together: sitting in silence. I knew that whenever one is invited to his table, he does not give space to the I's. Nothing unnecessary or trivial is uttered. If one ventures to say something just for the sake of starting a conversation, he does not acknowledge it.

That has always been tough but good, for it forces one to be in kings of centers while in his presence.

When one is in kings of centers one's steward has to get active, because the king of clubs itself gets very active. Things can become pretty tense then. Basically one has to be aware of these two forces within one, namely the nine of hearts and the nine of clubs. The nine of clubs is mechanically active, while the nine of hearts can only be stimulated by effort.

Because I was the only native speaker, I was asked to serve as an interpreter: take care of the orders, translate menus and when necessary, read maps and ask for directions to places. But Robert put a leash on that role, since, as I spoke my mother tongue, my attention easily slipped to the jacks. As soon as this happened I heard Robert's voice saying, "That's enough, Dear." Then I had to pay attention to what I said or did. I realized that in order to be of any service to Robert in the moment, I had to be alert and make the I's passive.

Presence is within grasp in this very favorable situation.

After breakfast Robert made a few calls and saw what the possibilities were for the day. From the beginning I noticed that he has no plan, and oftentimes not even his secretary knows what is going to happen next. There were several suggestions prepared for him beforehand

In Touch With The Miraculous

of things to do and places to go, but he did not decide until the last moment. How he decides I do not know. Once he had me make arrangements to visit a town he was interested in. I looked it up on the map, asked for directions and tips for possible short cuts, and when we got into the car he led the student who was driving into a totally different direction. Not a single word was spoken about my search.

That day we went to the Museum of Anthropology in Mexico City and Robert asked me what I wished to see. I said the Maya and he then decided that we would go to see the Aztec. As we went in, he asked me a few questions about the Sun Stone, also known as the Aztec Calendar. He listened to my explanations very attentively, so attentively that it was very shocking to see him actually paying attention to me and what I was saying in the moment. The quality of attention he directed towards me was not only focused on the information I had to share with him, but more importantly on the part of me that was addressing him in the moment. That was somewhat scary for the lower self but ultimately sobering for me. And it was one of the things I most appreciated in him; for he was forcing me to see in the moment what device within me was addressing him. It was like being carefully observed through a magnifying glass, literally.

After he listened to a few of my explanations, he asked me to help him find objects that he could use to illustrate his teaching events. All of us in fact started to look for useful images. Every time one suggested something, one had to do it in a detached way, because sometimes Robert

Fragments Of An Enduring Teaching

agreed with our observations and asked whoever was available to take a picture of the object in view, but often he just ignored whatever we had to show him.

The aim is to find objects that illustrate a silent reality, but one has to "BE" that silent reality in order to find a work of art that may help others remember it. Mesoamerican art can be shocking but very direct in its message. We took a lot of successful images from it.

One has to be present as one exposes oneself to a work of art and sees how it can be useful. Whenever one stops making an effort to be present, the whole activity becomes a moving center exercise, looking for similarities and correspondences. Sometimes the lower self sends the I's that say this is a ridiculous endeavor, especially if one is knowledgeable in the area. Since I have read a number of books on Mesoamerica, and being of Nahua origin, my lower self is pretty much involved in the subject. Several times I told Robert that what he was seeing was "actually not what he thought but something else"; yet he would quickly photograph me, "You are just talking about it, Dear. Let's see what we can find."

Robert is a master in the art of turning anything he wishes into a work "I". Like the sun, he makes the dawn wherever he appears.

One has to be very simple and detached from one's opinions if one wishes to participate in finding images that can be useful for our Teacher's task. When one has a direct personal experience of the silent reality he is trying to reveal, one will find a suitable image. Otherwise one is just trying to please him and missing the point.

Robert is only pleased by presence.

==

One of the things worthy of notice is that every time I fell into imagination, Robert found a way to pull me back, sometimes by asking me to do something: count objects, take a photo of something, or go for an errand, yet other times by pointing at something in the environment. These were just pretexts to call me back to the moment, for the fact is that when he called me back from a higher state wherein he lives it was presence calling the steward back to work.

==

Robert does not travel for leisure; he is always at work during the day. Either he is on the phone with the people involved in octaves in progress, or studying new ideas to implement at Apollo. Both lunch and dinner are experiences that fit this aspect of his work. I noticed this only the second day, when he insisted that I taste food from the others at the table instead of having just my usual salad. He finally suggested that I order this or that dish and pass it around for sharing. It was more of a tasting experience. Of course the lower self found it extremely difficult to go out of patterns in relation to one of its main identifications, food. But I made a deal with it saying that we would fast the day we returned home, and then go back to normal.

Robert not only tastes everything attentively, but encourages one to taste and enjoy one's food. He really enjoys tasting good food and good margaritas, but he does not get lost in the experience. He simply eats when he eats and makes the best out of it. But all does not end there, for he tries to see if it is possible to repeat the same dishes at our restaurant at Apollo. In fact a few new recipes are now being tested by our main chef, Alicia. For this purpose I had to constantly deal with servers asking them in detail how food was prepared and what was in each plate. I consulted with the servers over and over trying to figure out how a particular dish was made. At some moment a lady waitress got really impatient and asked me why these people were so picky with their food, and why they needed to know in detail what they were eating. I told her that Robert was a master cook and the rest were his apprentices. He was teaching them how to taste and I was simply a translator. Then her attitude changed. She became more efficient and respectful.

===

Our visit to Monte Alban in the state of Oaxaca is worthy of notice, because I had visited the site several times during the growth of my magnetic center. There I experienced Higher Forces as a tangible reality some thirty years ago. Additionally, when Robert went there for the first time a couple of years ago he had his secretary call me and mentioned that some of the conscious beings that had built the site visited him. That was pretty remarkable since I had experienced the same, but never mentioned it to him. The place may create the third state in one. But this time I entered the site in a third state already, Robert's hand holding my arm. I was genuinely happy and somewhat perplexed to be walking in presence with a conscious being in a place I had come to looking for a conscious being. I mentioned this to Robert and he quickly replied, "You were looking for your Self."

Later on he asked his scribe on duty to write down the following words, "When one is looking for a school, one is, in fact, looking for one's Self. A teacher is ineffective if the students fail to look for their own third eye."

On the way back to the city of Oaxaca he asked me how my experience at Monte Alban was after thirty years. "The same", I replied.

=======================================

We stayed in Oaxaca for a few days and visited a couple of museums. One afternoon, as we were having coffee at the main piazza, a man approached us with great surprise and exclaimed, "Hello, I know you! I visited Apollo and I had a very nice time there! I have been here for three weeks now." Everybody at the table tried to recognize his face. After a while nobody could really tell who he was, so he moved away, almost embarrassed. Later on we figured out he was a former student, but no name came to mind; probably someone who joined and left straight away. During the whole incident Robert did not even acknowledge him. He just continued sipping his coffee and remained silent about the matter until more or less dinner time. Then he remarked, "If he did not recognize influence C before, he will not recognize it now. I wonder if Higher Forces are giving him a second chance."

The paradox that made this a significant shock is that Oaxaca is known as a place where one can encounter what in the Toltec tradition is known as a "man of knowledge" or a shaman. During his trip to this particular place this former student came face to face with a conscious living teacher he had previously met, and failed to recognize.

======================================

As we traveled from Oaxaca back to Mexico City we stopped in Puebla. There we went to visit the Amparo Museum, where Robert had previously found many images for his events. We were extremely tired when we got there, so we were not getting anything out of the exhibition. We were just dragging our bodies through the various rooms. Everybody was trying to suggest this or that image to pick, but we were not working from the right level of attention. Robert noticed this soon enough and walked away from us. He was visibly tired. Some of us went on through the rest of the rooms without much success and then went to meet Robert at the cafeteria. He had gone to the gift shop to buy a hat for a student. I saw him getting up from his chair, restored and ready to keep making efforts, but we did not go back to see the exhibition.

A few times I noticed that when he did not have the right

energy to work, he did not hesitate to stop whatever activity he was engaged in and focused on recovering his strength in order to continue working. He sometimes moved onto a completely different activity if necessary. In this case we had traveled to the city of Puebla to visit this particular museum. The trip was long and tiring. Yet we just dropped the activity completely when he noticed we were not getting anywhere. We went shopping for white socks instead, which by the way was a memorable episode.

His focus is on trying to be present; the rest is secondary. This is one of the main working standards I learned from him; that is, the priority to reach a higher state and stay there, and restore it when it is fading. He made **that** practical for me.

A real Teacher silently transmits his inner discipline.

One morning I was waiting at the hotel restaurant for others to join me, when Sasha came and told me Robert was at a nearby mall in Starbucks waiting for us. So I canceled the table, got a few of his favorite pastries and joined him there. When I arrived he was reading some papers, and the others were at their computers. His secretary was busy going in and out of the coffee shop running errands. I sat in silence. His phone kept ringing. Every once in a while he would ask a student to check his emails. I was not asked to do anything, so I just sat there assuming we would leave any moment after breakfast. At some point the lower self became irritated and started to produce negative I's about Robert and the whole trip.

Everybody was going around doing errands and I was just sitting there. At times there was only the two of us sitting in silence, I was struggling with impatience. This went on for two long hours. All I could do was try to relax and be present for I did not have an assigned activity.

Finally I decided to walk around the mall and see if there was a bookstore or something to browse. Just then Robert told me to follow him and help him get a haircut in a beauty parlor at the mall. "Come dear, I want to work with you now", he said. That was a most intense experience, because by then I was very close to the third state, and relaxed. As we entered the parlor I translated his needs and sat down nearby in case he needed me. I took one of the magazines and pretended to be looking at it, but in effect I was just being present to this curious situation. Robert was looking at himself in the mirror. He was looking at himself as if he were looking at somebody else.

Presence is so simple.

When we came out of the beauty parlor, he grabbed my arm and asked me about Jose Antonio Kahuil. I told him how he had used marijuana and peyote as tools to teach me higher possibilities. His comments on the subject surprised me, and for that reason they remain clear in my memory, but I am still digesting the information. He was leaning towards me as he spoke softly. I was witnessing the shrine of his presence. There was a soft pulsation within my solar plexus; and then I realized my own presence was within a shrine: the nine of hearts combusting became a living reality.

In Touch With The Miraculous

What makes these fine interactions with Robert possible is one's ability to sustain a higher state on a regular basis. Robert's being cannot be easily grasped.

==

The lower self resented having to travel under such continuous pressure. It seems to it that Robert is just a man who does whatever he wants and one has to comply with that. Of course the lower self does not read Robert from the point of view of the Work but of advantage and disadvantage. Although it did not express it openly during the day, early in the morning it tried to introduce I's to keep me out of the traveling crew. By the end of the trip a couple of times it thought to just call them and tell them I wanted to be by myself for a while, because I was not feeling well or something.

But I did not listen to those I's.

The last night we spent together he asked me, "How did you like the journey, dear?" "Robert", I said, "To travel with you is to travel at the speed of light."

Never missing a beat, he said, smiling, "We are just trying to be present here."

Influence C was influence C when it was given and in the circumstances it was given.
Rodney Collin

Final note

When interacting with a conscious being one has to keep in mind what one wishes to learn from him. If all one wishes is his sympathy, he will give one his sympathy. If one wishes to be selected for a role, or a task, he will find it for one. But when one's aim is to become a conscious being, he will provide the circumstances for one to achieve that. However he cannot make efforts for one.

The lower self sees Robert as a rascal and a trouble maker or simply as the owner of a curious circus; whereas the divinity within one recognizes the divinity within Robert Burton and its power.

Our lives and School are in the hands of Higher Forces. They have brought us all together; they will keep us together or disperse us if necessary. They have given us this very simple System which works when we use it, and they could have given us any other system or method. Every ordinary man and woman in this School who is making the right efforts is moving toward permanent self awareness, one effort at a time. Like in any nursery, every one is cared for by invisible gardeners. Without Higher Forces no one can awaken.

We are lucky to have been brought to work together.

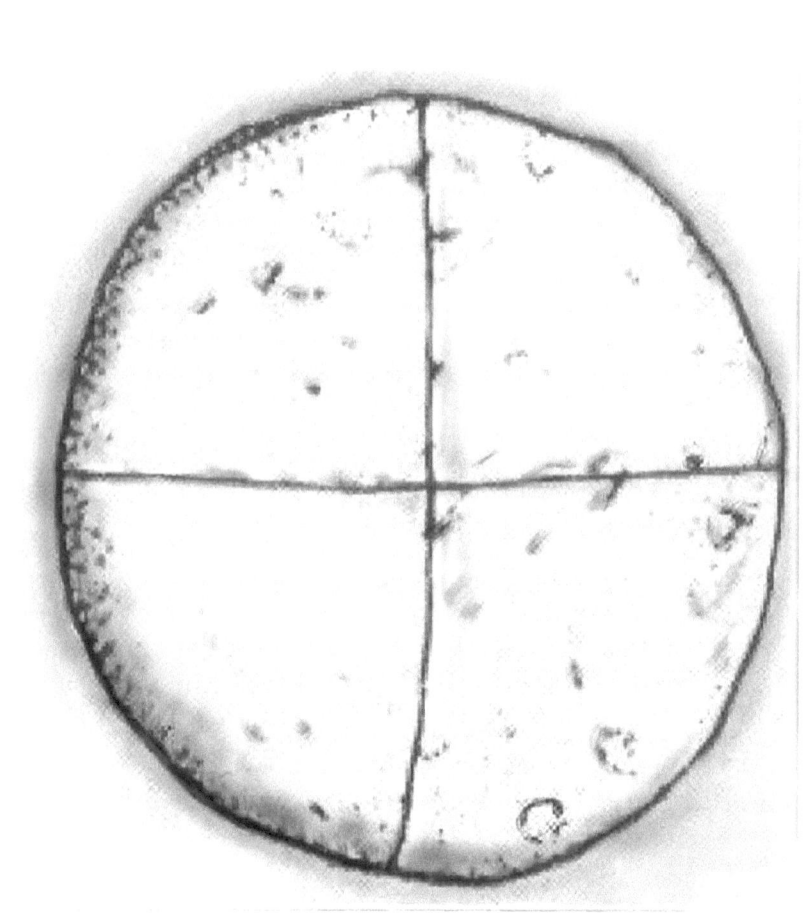

Appendix: A Further Effort

Written notes are no music until they find a voice.
Christina Rossetti

The following document, "A Further Effort", was printed separately a year before the first publication of "Living the Miraculous". It seems pertinent to include it here since it shows how Robert Burton facilitated the refinement of this teaching to its essentials. The document also describes a period in the development of our School when a door was open for some, while remaining closed for others.

The notes need no prologue, as they will speak for themselves to those for whom they are intended. We know well that the ideas they contain are not ours, they are School ideas squeezed through us. Finally, words are barren if they do not come from action, and lead to action.

With love and gratitude,

Rolando Altamirano

The Sequence is a reflection of prehistoric man. Its simplicity had to arise from such a psychology. One can awaken without the Sequence; however, the Sequence is a perfected school method for awakening.
Robert

I

Whenever he interacts with students, the Teacher introduces shocks that puzzle our lower centers and help Presence emerge in us. In the past, at dinner, he used to throw a bun across the table to a student; and then he would remark: "this state is your Self." Of course neither the shock nor the statement guaranteed the experience of one's Self, since at times this shock caught one so asleep that it simply caused one to laugh and loose the opportunity to make an effort.

One time I was able to make a conscious effort after Robert threw a piece of bread across the table during dinner. I suddenly felt a higher hydrogen circulating within my body, and noticed it slowly fading away as Robert went on saying "This is your Self". I made the effort to keep quiet until finally Presence emerged. It was a surprise to see the I's of the moment dispelled for a few seconds, yet my will did not hold long. I did not have a precise work "I" to help me prolong the experience; I simply tried to remain present in silence for as long as possible... I do not remember the moment when I fell asleep again.

For a long time most of our efforts were sporadic, and typically related to moments of friction or when external stimuli generated energy within the machine. As a School we did not have a tool, or a method to introduce and sustain Presence when it was produced by a shock from our Teacher, Influence C, the law of accident, or fate... Of course we did not have a method to promote Presence on a regular basis and in relatively neutral moments.

II

We have recently been given a method that successfully increases our moments of Presence: this method is the Sequence. It was not given to us for free, or all at once, but it was developed through effort in a slow and organized way. Of course Robert had the vision that such method was needed, (Ouspensky did too) and had developed many exercises to help us introduce Presence during the day.

For example, before the Sequence, a method was devised to check the amount of times we actually make the effort to be present, by means of a small counting device we kept in our pockets. We needed to click it every time we made the effort. The aim was to do it at least one hundred times a day. This experiment was very successful for it allowed us to verify the frequency of our efforts, but it did not help us test their depth or duration. The experiment ended when the lower self got accustomed to it and simply led us into the illusion that we were making a fruitful effort every time we clicked. Eventually it became entirely mechanical and was removed.

Later on the Teacher decided to make a list of the fourteen

best ways to remember one's self, taking into account the most recurrent circumstances in which we could make that effort. Although the list was developed by Robert, he did ask for students' suggestions. As he developed these methods, he kept introducing exercises that even now help us control attention in the emotional center, the most successful of them being the control of wit. This exercise proved to be a leash for the lower self, since it reduced the space it took in most of our interactions with students.

Soon after, we engaged in the development of a list of the most effective thirty work I's that could help us introduce and prolong Presence on a regular basis. We did not just try to figure out which thirty work I's would best help us introduce Presence, but we actually developed several lists and tested them; and observed in our everyday experience what was missing or could be improved.

Only in the end, when we had come to define the most effective thirty Work I's, the idea of repeating them in a Sequence came to us. I don't remember how we chose the term "Sequence" amongst others, but we had learned by then, that other schools and traditions had some kind of practice similar to what we had discovered through our study and course of action. Some schools called their Sequence a prayer, others a mantra, a chant or some kind of ritual repetition that would help to dismiss the thousands of I's produced by the lower self.

Some sacred texts indeed refer to such effort as a sequence.

III

As we were trying to develop this method to awaken, we engaged in a particular line of work. At Robert's request, we scanned all kinds of texts and art which any of us thought contained the hidden message of using the physical body as a mechanism that could be used to reach the state of Divine Presence. We came across many schools, traditions and individuals who actually engaged in the same, if not a similar effort.

The development of the Sequence was an organized effort made through our School all over the world that lasted quite some time. Many students participated actively in it. Robert often said at meetings that at least two thirds of the material and observations that he shared came from his students. He never said it was his own invention, and we know it was not: he was simply grateful to Influence C for having given us such a privilege. Those who participated in the process, directly or indirectly, saw clearly the work of higher forces in the creation of the Sequence.

IV

Recently a student said that she experienced a sudden attack of negative I's. It went on and on for a while until, at some point, her emotional center awoke and started saying, "Help me God, to get rid of these I's. I do not want them." And then she went to get a book and started reading in order to raise her level of attention.

This is a good example of a moment when the steward

suddenly awakens and sees the lower self in total control of our ruling faculty, but the level of attention is not exactly the nine of hearts. We all have had many moments like this one. But now, instead of crying "Help me God, to get rid of these I's, I do not want them", we have a more harmonious effort to introduce in such moments. What is more, the same effort can be applied in most circumstances in our lives, regardless of their nature, and the result of such effort is to arrive to a state where we remain undisturbed, this state is Divine Presence.

Our efforts are still dim, like dawn, we are simply learning to say "Be", "Hold".

V

One will have difficulty relating to the Sequence if one does not practice it. If left as a theory, the Sequence is just a mechanical repetition of syllables which can turn one into a robot. Just like the nine of hearts, when seen as a concept, and not as an effort to control attention, it has no practical meaning. Anyway, one who does not practice, will fail to see that the new effort we are undertaking is based on the same system we all learned from Ouspensky and Gurdjieff; that is, we are working on controlled attention and divided attention.

The Sequence is an entirely new line of effort granted to our School because we are ready for it.

VI

Some of our friends are leaving the School due to the fact that they cannot relate to the Sequence and Robert's presentation of diverse teachings of the past. How can one abandon the Work just when one is given a more precise and effective method of awakening? This is the result of lack of preparatory work. That is, he who did not spend the last years of his life creating a deputy steward and a steward, cannot start working with the Sequence successfully: for only the steward can recognize the Sequence as a powerful tool and work with it.

In the past, the steward had, and still has, a variety of tools to lift the veil of imagination, transform negativity, and prepare the way for the emergence of Presence. But we have arrived at the point where the steward must be willing and able to engage Presence practically in any moment, or as the Sufi would say, attain instant Union with the Beloved. That is why it consists of six work I's only. The rest of the tools the steward still uses we call "'I's related to promoting Presence". But a lot of old tools now have become obsolete. Working with the Sequence is not as hard for new students, since when one finds a conscious teaching, one is open and enthusiastic to start working with anything that might increase one's chances of becoming conscious.

In a way, all the work done before new students joined, is acting as a shortcut for them. They do not need to study the system as a whole, like for example, learning to distinguish between functions and types, or about considering. Now they are simply being led to the door where all our previous efforts have brought us: the nine of hearts, where the Sequence is born. Of course the background of the system is also available for anyone to study; it is just that we no longer spend much time with it.

VII

It is written somewhere that at some point Ouspensky said he would abandon the system. Well, it is not the case with Robert. He did not abandon the system: as a master of refinement, he simply distilled the system to its essentials.

VIII

One can see the Sequence as a series of promptings intoned from the level of attention we call the nine of hearts, in order to remember to be present to the activity of the moment: for example, the work 'I' "Taste" especially means "remember the Divinity within you as you taste food", "divide your attention". The effort is not simply to pay attention to what one is doing, but to divide attention as one does it. It does not mean for example, "Taste your food Rolando" -because Rolando ill more or less taste its food and eat it anyway. It means instead, "awake within the physical body", "appear and be present to what is happening now."

This is the reason why we always start with "Be", since Presence has to emerge in the midst of mechanical activity, and "Be" must persist in every work "I" of the Sequence. The Sequence is the longing for the Beloved, a prayer to reach God, the effort to be aware of the Divinity within; Robert refers to it as the effort to engage Presence.

IX

When Presence emerges, the lower self becomes alarmed, and it gets active, diligently sending one "I" after another, an endless chain of options to put Presence back to sleep.

The lower self is always here, aloof, biding its time. When one keeps the effort to intone the Sequence, the I's suggested by the lower self are seen for what they are.

Although the lower self cannot be present, it is in the present, optimizing its chances to keep us immersed in imagination. The lower self is said to be the king of the jungle. This means that, being the part of the machine which is conscious of itself, it knows it very well: its wants, its needs, and inclinations. It knows very well how to keep he machine working on its own devices and drive the steward out. In this case, we could unmistakably say that the lower self is mostly "Rolando". The steward, in turn, is an impersonal device, comprised of six syllables only, and is born from the level of attention of the nine of hearts. This level of attention is very difficult to achieve and sustain.

X

Even though since the beginning I was positive about the use of the Sequence, I could not introduce it successfully. Until one time, as I attended a dinner with Robert, I came into direct contact with the Presence of higher centers within me, as well as the definite feeling of the nine of hearts becoming active.

At this point I had the urge to practice the work 'I' "Be" as I felt the Presence of higher centers. I simply attached the word "Be" to the experience. Right then I clearly saw the lower self becoming active, suggesting a subject of interest. Then "Hold" fell in the right place, since Presence had already emerged. Then I kept on knitting "Look"; slowly intoning the Sequence as I was certain of Presence.

Presence is not Rolando; Rolando is clearly the world, the seventy two nations. Presence is truly God, Allah, the Lord of Intimate Vicinity. Thus the steward is clearly Christ, Mohamed, Arjuna, Robert within one.

XI

When Robert started teaching again we did not have the Sequence. We just attended events with the understanding that, when we make the effort, something of a higher nature can manifest within us during this time. This effort on our side was to try and keep the I's quiet before and during the event; but the higher state produced then did not last long. The lower self quickly regained its domain through imagination, haste, negativity, etc.

The Sequence is a precise method that allows us to return to the state we experience while in the Presence of our friends and our dear Teacher. Yet it is necessary to have experienced that state often enough and to know that THIS is exactly what we desire; for how can you fall in love with someone you have never met; or whom you see only once in a blue moon?

XII

Students wish to sincerely intone the Sequence, but some still have not found a way to make it work, either because English is not their native language or because they cannot associate it to an inner action of spiritual nature in themselves. That is, something they have tried in the past in order to come in contact with the Divinity within. Perhaps they still do not relate to the term "Sequence" as a series of efforts intended to reach a higher state. In that case it is pertinent to suggest them to see the Sequence as a more effective way to introduce and sustain divided attention.

Some manage to see the Sequence as a form of prayer, meditation, penitence, mantra, or Self Remembering while raising the level of attention to the kings of centers. In any case, the "Sequence" requires Self Remembering: It is Self Remembering applied to its full depth and duration.

XIII

I understand the urgency to attend as many events with the Teacher as possible. These events offer the right atmosphere to evoke higher centers. Through a special effort, we may grasp the self-same taste of Presence. Additionally, we can compare that experience to the results of our daily work, for when we stand in Robert's Presence, we see the measure of our efforts made in solitude.

I find it useful to practice the Sequence in these ideal conditions in order to get the taste of the toil and the fruit of our labor. Together with this, we must have the aim to intone the Sequence as soon as we realize Presence is fading, (this usually happens as we walk out of an event) in order to create continuity. Because the lower self wants to make our work first intermittent and then occasional in order to create the illusion that we are working.

XIV

When I came in contact with the System ideas, a student suggested to keep the king of hearts card in my pocket and try to study that aspect of the machine until I clearly understood what "king of hearts" means. It took some time before I understood that "king of hearts" means controlled attention in the emotional center. Something very difficult to achieve and, as far as I can tell, it has not become mechanical.

Similarly we have to experiment with the work "I" "Be"

as we try to be present; until we manage to marry the utterance with the emergence of Presence. "Be" must act as a wake up call for Presence and a rein for the lower self. Sometimes we do not reach Presence, but the steward is still intoning a Sequence, bringing us to a state where we allow no I's, but Presence does not appear. I believe this is the state our Anonymous English Monk calls the "Cloud of Unknowing"; that is, a state were we relinquish the world, but we are still not in the Presence of God. We are invoking God from this cloud of not-knowing: the Sequence takes place there... the second state.

Faith and doubt must coexist in silence, protected by the heart.

XV

There are times when the lower self becomes aware of itself and calls it Presence, but the taste is distinctive, since it also contains the feeling of being separate from others, or being the only one present in the room; anyway one feels rather stiff. Also, Presence modifies the molecular configuration of the machine, and the lower self records that; later on it imitates the experience in order to fool us into thinking that Presence is at hand.

Once we are certain that Presence has emerged, "Hold" makes perfect sense.

Also, the lower self often starts a Sequence of its own without choosing a theme, it does this with the intention of creating the illusion of work, while jamming the

Sequence every time. A permanent aim is to establish a theme for every situation.

A well poised candle performs its task completely.

XVI

There are moments and circumstances when the lower self is not as strong, so we must put ourselves in such circumstances. Spending time with students who are focused always works.

XVII

Yesterday, just before the meeting I was struggling with a fierce negative emotion, and it would not go away by solely using the work "I" "Peace". The lower self was quite strong. I had to introduce a series of Sequences, using "Peace" as theme, in order to simply assert and sustain the power of the steward. After a series of efforts the hydrogen of the negative emotion finally transformed into Presence. Once the negative emotion subsided, I returned to "Look" as the theme of the Sequence. The residue of negativity was dealt with a simple "Peace". I must say, because I was at the meeting, the steward was strong.

XVIII

The battle has become quite clear. When the Teacher is present, I have to be present; otherwise someone else is active pretending it is I, and it is mostly puzzled by the

Teacher's Presence and words. Our Teacher is a master in the art of jamming the lower functions. He often says things, or does things that are indigestible for them. This is the perfect ground for Presence to appear, but we must make the effort to engage. It is exactly in these circumstances when we must say "Be", "Hold", and be grateful that the Teacher has shaken our sleep. We do not know how lucky we are if we do not realize that this is a gift. The question is not whether or not Robert's words make sense, but that he is giving us the tools and the environment to actually awaken in the moment.

XIX

Robert teaches in the molecular world, whenever one is present, one may receive and apply his message, whenever one is not present, one is in imagination about the whole thing, positive or negative is all the same.

XX

Students lose the School when they cease to understand its nature, that is, it is esoteric, occult, and it is recognizable solely through the constant practice of its principles. In other words, it is only recognizable by one who is present or making the effort to be present. When there is no effort, there is no school. We must not forget the principle that the School is real only when one is real. Whenever one stops making efforts, the clock strikes twelve and Cinderella is in rags again.

XXI

We are very lucky that we can serve God by an act of will in the moment.

XXII

The lower self does not want the steward to become wise, for that will diminish its power. It awakes before dawn, with a clear agenda. Thus we must also have an agenda: pocket size, and make the aim to rise early and check out what the lower self is up to.

XXIII

We have to get tired of living in suspense and step into Presence, again and again until it becomes a permanent state.

XXIV

The Sequence is to be persistently introduced during the day; as no garden is totally free from weeds. Now, we used to weed by hand, the Sequence is more like "Round-Up".

XXV

We developed the Sequence as a method to return to ourselves every time we get distracted, but we are discovering that we were more distracted than we suspected.

When we are distracted, the lower self does its best to deny it. It wants to keep the steward in a hamster wheel.

XXVI

One must not fool oneself into thinking that one is unique

or different, for we all share the same enemy, we all share the same aim and the thirty work I's are the same for all. Finally, Presence is the same in all and everywhere.

XXVII

A student suggested today that as a School, we are now working at the level of man number five, having to transform so much friction moment by moment- this friction being simply to give up the "I" of the moment. With the Sequence, the steward has the lower self cornered, and like a cornered beast, the lower self is in the act of launching a brutal attack, that is why so many of us are falling.

XXVIII

Robert has always acted intentionally toward his students, mostly shocking our lower centers in order to create the right inner atmosphere for higher centers to emerge; he does so in many different ways. But the fact remains that only one who understands the nature and purpose of his shocks, is always in the position of working with them. His work in this area is intended to release energy which is locked and checked by the lower self. In the past he used to do this mainly with students that happened to have direct contact with him, and now he is doing it for the School as a whole. There have always been two main aspects of his teaching, one to remind students, time after time, to be present, to divide attention, to invoke the Divinity within, and the second to create the necessary conditions to bring us closer to the shore of awakening.

The shore of awakening is controlled attention.

Again, every time Robert provides a shock for any of us, it is meant to jam lower centers and prepare the ground for higher centers, but the effort to engage Presence is our responsibility alone. When we do not bring in some kind of conscious effort, the only experience left for us is the lower self distilling negativity. This is why the creation and nourishment of a steward is so necessary. Where there is no steward, there are no possibilities. One cannot digest, let alone transform, Robert's conscious influence unless one's steward is active.

XXIX

We do not go to events with the Teacher out of worship, but out of conviction; day after day we keep verifying and working with this system on our own.

XXX

Apollo is a truly spiritual dimension, and very few will find it, for it can only be reached and preserved through constant effort. The moment one stops making efforts, Apollo vanishes into imagination.

XXXI

When Presence emerges, there is no place for imagination or negative emotions in relation to people, life or oneself. This is the meaning of the idea that one's heart has to be as light as a feather in the "day of judgment". The emotional center has to simply be focused on promoting Presence.

XXXII

The work "I" "Hold" has the distinct quality of being in love and entreating the beloved to linger, only the nine of hearts can sing this song.

XXXIII

Being in kings of centers implies that the king of clubs is active too. The way to neutralize it is to acknowledge it and start a Sequence using a theme related to the activity of the moment. Presence will not disregard the lower self.

XXXIV

Those who plot the damage of a conscious school do not know that Presence cannot be damaged. Moreover, whatever action they take against it, only adds to its perfection.

XXXV

The Sequence is movement toward the invisible; the beginning of existence.

XXXVI

There is essentially nothing wrong with the lower self, it is our work that goes against its nature.

XXXVII

When the steward awakens soon after a violent negative emotion, he must act quickly on the feeling of shame and use it as fuel for the Sequence, for this feeling is quickly manipulated by the lower self. The work 'I' "Peace" can be used as the starting point for a few seconds. Nowadays I find it more successful to use "Look" or "Hear" as the theme; in order to prevent the lower from taking advantage of a moment of weakness and sink the steward deeper down.

The aim is to return to Presence untouched by emotions, including shame. Similarly when one finds oneself deep in imagination after a long period of time, one must not dwell on the feeling of time lost, but focus on the fact that one is suddenly awake and work from there.

The Sequence must be intoned at once until it restores Presence.

XXXVIII

The lower self loves playful interactions, as they are often meant to keep one relaxed, content and distracted. We have to learn to be more silent amongst us.

XXXIX

It has been said that we must learn to distinguish between the teacher and the person playing that role, similarly we must also learn to distinguish between the School and the organization we call the Fellowship of Friends. Since we are both, the School and the Fellowship of Friends, we can say that when we simply wish to hold on to a status within the organization, however humble or prominent, we are nothing more than the Fellowship of Friends. Yet when we are present or struggling to be present, we are the School: consciousness is not functions.

XL

"Put all these words into the mouth of your servant."[16] This probably refers to the fact that the Sequence is not one's own, but a prayer designed only to invoke the Divinity within. A student reminded us that when prayer becomes even slightly personal, we may suspect the lower self at work behind it.

XLI

We now recognize Presence as the "four wordless breaths"; this state is very similar to the way a new born looks at the world. One does not have I's then; for a brief moment one is clearly within a physical body, but one is not the body. When we were newborns we did not know that we were present, and now we know that we are present... the king of clubs knows this too.

---

16   Samuel 14:19

XLII

Today, anyone who wants can become a conscious being in our School. And anyone unable to say "I am actually becoming more awake" has to start doing something about it, because now it is possible to do something about it. After so many years of work, we have put ourselves in the position that we can "DO".

XLIII

We cannot spend time with former students. Our efforts united us, lack of effort divides us; we were friends in the work, not in the world.

XLIV

Our days are quite stressful, since we have to give up every "I" we observe as we focus our attention on the steward intoning the Sequence. We do not really exist unless Presence emerges: this truly means dying to the body before its death.

XLV

If there is such a thing as justice in our work, it must be that every one will reach as far as his own efforts take him.

XLVI

Anyone who has attempted any kind of prayer, spell or any form of Sequence to dispel imagination, has come face to face with the instinctive center and its schemes. That is why prayer must be kept short and simple.

XLVII

When we raise our level of attention in the emotional center, the nine of clubs becomes active. This is simply because when we raise our level of attention we are entering its territory. The king of clubs reserves controlled attention to circumstances and events that guarantee its supremacy over the machine and its environment.

XLVIII

Ever since I met Robert, I have seen him relentlessly inviting us to wake up and meet him in the present. Some students do wake up and find him quietly and powerfully seated in Presence. Some fail to wake up, and do not see him, then turn away irritated or disappointed. In those who do see him in the moment, two tendencies arise: one is fascination with the state produced by his Presence, which leads to some sort of addiction to the experience. The other one is a desire to follow his instructions in order to permanently join him in a higher world.

A voucher allows us to sit at his table, the Sequence allows us to sit with him in Presence.

XLIX

Robert has been very diligent in creating an ever-changing network of exercises that act as shocks and alarm clocks carefully placed within our every day environment. This is part of the magic of his teaching, wherever in the world one is, whatever situation one is in, there is always a reminder to return to the effort to engage Presence.

L

People who abandon the teaching ignore the fact that they decide to jump off a plane which is flying high up in the sky, and moving at an increasing speed: this simply means, they are truly left far behind. Those who jump rarely make it back.

LI

The essence of our work is to reach a higher state and remain there, undistracted: one who is present always and everywhere makes God omnipresent.

LII

It is quite a struggle to be present when the emergence of certain people or circumstances stimulates the lower self in all its strength. We have to start using the Sequence in areas like these, so far marked as the lower self's wild territory. Robert says the Sequence shows the shrewdness of the lower self, and it also shows us where we did not work before. Whenever we catch the lower self judging, we must step in and say "Drop", with the same energy that we use when land-clearing.

LIII

A long time ago, a student asked if in the School there existed some sort of sieve designed to shun the unwilling and the insincere. I now see that the sieve is built within each student's machine, it is called the chief feature, the source of resistance.

LIV

It is impossible to be fully awake and have accounts, for when we are present we see accounts are incompatible with the third state; just as weeds are incompatible with the beauty of a garden.

LV

It takes a lot of energy and little effort to argue with the teacher's instructions, and it takes much effort but less energy to follow them.

LVI

In prayer, the nature of the vessel determines the quality of the substance it holds. Let's not pray with the moving center.

LVII

The School is so elusive that many people simply come and go without noticing it. They are like a man in a museum walking through the exhibitions failing to stop his inner dialogue in order to be exposed to what is in there, and finally stepping out the door with some opinion of the experience. On the other hand, some students are specifically summoned to join the School and enter its invisible realm. Those students carry the School within even before they meet the Teacher. The School is the garden, the park of abundance where every flower, every palm tree, every sculpture, every fountain has been carefully chosen, brought and put in place with great love and effort.

LVIII

In order to meet the teacher in the moment, one has to make it through the narrow gate; there is no other way of seeing who he is. Naturally, once one is there, one also understands who one is... then all is well.

LVIX

I used to believe that if one makes the right efforts, one may become eternal after death. Robert has shown us and keeps reminding us to become eternal now. It is possible. "... willpower is now or never..."

LX

The steward, like a good servant, must always be at hand and never in the way.

LXI

One has to have a magnetic center, or a steward, active and strong, otherwise the School will be of no use to one, even if one proves to be exceptionally useful for the School.

LXII

Desire for union with the Divine is ignited within the nine of hearts by the Divine itself. God wishes to see himself in us. He lifts the veil and reveals himself within us, just for a brief moment, thus stirring our desire to call him back and dwell within us evermore. The Sequence is indeed a love song, but it has to be felt and sung with Love and great humility. On the other hand, desire for union in the physical world is born within the physical body, and has as its aim the preservation of the physical world. When the lower self experiences union with its complementary part, fulfillment of this union is the perpetuation of its features in its kin: this surrogate of eternity is all it desires.

LXIII

The School exists in our ten inner actions.

LXIV

When the lower self experiences small irritations and becomes active, I apply "Use" as theme. It takes time before the hydrogen is transformed. When I reappear from imagination as I drive, I introduce "Turn" to refocus and then start a Sequence using "Look' or "Hear".

LXV

Robert often states that ever since he started working with the Sequence, he unveiled the treacherous nature of the lower self. I agree with him, so far it remained mostly undisturbed, and that is why many of us were stuck in relative awakening for so long.

LXVI

Through great effort we come to the narrow gate; there we must not hesitate to drop the last of our baggage, lest the door is shut again. The baggage might be as light as a thought, as swift as an impression.

LXVII

The aim of our Work is to become part of the conscious aspects of the ray of creation. The Sequence we have been given is a method to fulfill that, not an end in itself. I agree with Robert's statement that one can become conscious without it. However if it helps us become conscious in the moment, I do not see why not use it. It is a tool granted to the steward, and the steward is the result of will.

LXVIII

Pursuing virtue for its sake will only lead us to some kind of conventional conduct, and eventually to self delusion. Virtue comes as a result of Presence. We pursue Presence, and when we reach that state, no evil or impurity can come forth from our nine of hearts, for evil happens when we lose attention. As our nine of hearts remains active during Presence, all our thoughts, feelings and actions abide by virtue... we are entering the state that proves there is no conscious evil. As Presence becomes more permanent, virtue becomes voluntary.

LXIX

We are now like Ali Baba, at the mouth of the cave, waiting and willing to say, "Open Sesame". Ali Baba is controlled attention.

LXX

We used to work on ourselves by keeping our attention on the lower self while separating our identity from it, now we focus on the Presence alone, and we keep one "I" on the lower self: "Back".

LXXI

The Sequence is an act of will, the lower self cannot relate to it. It is meant to help you awaken, but it cannot guarantee anything. How can anyone guarantee your own efforts?

LXXIII

I am relieved to know that "to repent from sin" only means return from imagination and start a Sequence. Again, our aim and good fortune is to reach a higher state, stay there longer than possible, and restore it as soon as we notice we have lapsed.

LXXIV

The more we experience the third state of consciousness, the more we find the second state a dull place. In the second state our awareness is tossed to and fro by all kinds of distractions. The lower self (we used to call it the devil) is the manipulator of such distractions. It has been pointed out that it does not really care what subject he uses to distract us, as long as he gets us distracted. Now, we have to be direct and restore Presence right away, the Sequence is very effective.

LXXV

Robert is the merchant who sells good fortune; it is amazing how few can afford his ware.

LXXVI

Our inclination must be always to go uphill, and we must not turn back, he who goes downhill speeds as he descends.

LXXVII

Before intoning the Sequence, we must form the habit of bringing ourselves back to the level of attention of the nine of hearts: our love song must have that foundation.

Not many people are centered in the nine of hearts, and even those centered in that card will surely have difficulty asserting the power of the Sequence from that level of attention. The nine of hearts, as a mechanical device, is interested in lofty subjects, or in beauty, but it is not naturally inclined to intone a Sequence. It has to be instructed to do so.

Whoever has been touched from above must permanently shift their center of gravity to the nine of hearts and work from there. I doubt this will ever become mechanical.

LXXVIII

Higher Forces exist now, but lower centers are not sensitive to them. Thus Higher Forces will manipulate the physical world in order to reach us through lower centers, from the moment we meet them our life becomes a series of symbols that reveal a wordless state. Just like Higher Forces, our dear Teacher uses words and images to reach Higher Centers. Lower centers cannot be taught to be present, Presence itself has to be summoned by an act of magic; and our Teacher is certainly a magician.

LXXIX

Visible beauty may unveil invisible beauty for a split second: yet the steward must act upon the hydrogen with special attention and not let the lower self get involved: "Back" is to be intoned with firmness. This rare opportunity is a fleeting gift, for visible beauty is gone tomorrow, invisible beauty once raised and held, stays here and now forever.

LXXX

Meteor showers, moon phases, planetary tensions, all those mechanical influences serve as weights for the steward to create muscle. The time has come when everything encourages our work.

LXXXI

It is necessary to introduce the Sequence in circumstances other than events, when we know the steward is strong. Around students we tend to have the impulse to raise our level of attention, to be in kings of centers. It might just start with the moving center; that is, acquiring a more intentional posture and body language. Although this impulse is still mechanical, it puts us in the king of spades. Since the kings of centers work in unison, the steward can be brought forth from there, and of course, the king of clubs goes: Fee-fi-fo-fum!

LXXXII

The aim is not essence in idleness but Divine Presence embracing essence. It is fine to be a rivulet, as long as we flow into the ocean.

LXXXIII

The Sequence has put everybody at square one. And what is more, it has put one in direct contact with the amount of one's previous efforts.

LXXXIV

When we catch ourselves drowning in a negative emotion, or deep in imagination, chances are our steward has been inactive for a while. In our absence the lower self has got the time to organize a bacchanal. Our steward then, has to act like Jesus firing the money lenders from the temple.

LXXXV

We have to get used not to take personally the thoughts and feelings coming from the lower self; this, in the beginning is a mere mental, uncomfortable exercise. It has to be practiced as preparation for Presence, for when we reach Presence and we exist separate from the lower self, we see all mechanical thoughts and feelings as its devices to keep Presence veiled. We do not have to wait for death to prove that the I's produced within our bodies are mere illusions.

LXXXVI

The lower self always offers resistance to attend meetings. But we go anyway; there is no more negotiating with the lower self, we simply say "Be!" with conviction and the waters must become calm ...this is part of the magic we all experience nowadays.

LXXXVII

The Lower self can't bear Presence, because Presence proves that its existence is illusory and temporary. Fame, recognition, and offspring are its surrogates of eternity, just as interests, possessions and mechanical inclinations are its surrogates of reality. Presence has always been and will always be. It simply reappears within the physical body with great effort. The moments of memory we experienced early in our lives, which are of exactly the same nature as the ones we experience now, prove that Presence has always been here. During these moments we realize we are peeping into the present from another dimension.

LXXXVIII

When Presence first appears it creates the magnetic center within the machine; and with the help of influence C, it develops it into a steward. The steward then recognizes its like in other vessels, this is the moment when we find the School, not to be confused with the day we joined the Fellowship.

Influence C created our School because they understand the necessity to launch and maintain a continuous, organized effort to provide the right conditions for Presence to emerge.

LXXXIX

When we interact with "life people" it becomes evident that the enemy of our life is within. We are committed to a specific kind of effort of which they are unaware. We call them "life people" simply because they are mainly involved in life and its well-being, and there is nothing wrong with that.

Although former students do not enter the same category; we can no longer expect any kind of effort from them. In any case, we do not expect Presence to originate outside of ourselves, each one of us has learned to love the effort to return to work.

XC

In order to bring ourselves to the narrow gate, the very moment we reappear, we simply start paying attention to what the machine has been occupied with. If it is not related to awakening, a strong "Drop" or "Turn" may be sufficient to start controlling our attention. However, in some circumstances returning to work may seem more difficult than in others. However we do not see circumstances as difficult in themselves; we know that what makes them difficult is that the lower self has a definite attitude towards them. In such cases, "Back", is the starting effort to raise our attention. Our attention, however, is directed toward refining the quality of our feelings, not toward what the lower self intends. For he is a devious creature and will want to have us argue with him: our aim is to arrive at the narrow gate, not to have a talk with the devil.

XCI

Life has to sleep, for in waking it would see its utter nothingness, and that would be catastrophic.

XCII

The four wordless breaths, like an even snowfall, cloak the world in perfect silence.

XCIII

We acknowledge the lower self and keep an eye on it: "Back". A short thought is a shortcut.

XCIV

It is useful to know the machine's chief feature, and find a theme that applies to it.

XCV

In the past, when an "I" appeared within my field of awareness and was recognized as a distraction from the lower self, I used to introduce a work "I" given to me long ago: "not right now"; these days "Back" has replaced it.

XCVI

I wonder what consequences Christ had to deal with when he put his Lord Prayer into practice for the first time. The purpose of the Sequence or any sincere prayer is to restore the Presence of God within us, again and again. We are grateful to have been granted such privilege.

XCVII

Every time Influence C gives us a shock, they want to awake the steward so it starts making efforts to engage Presence. The lower self is very quick in reacting to these shocks; it scurries into our ears and suggests its own interpretation of the shock in order to make sense of it in terms of its existence; then move on to imagination about it.

XCVIII

The mind is process oriented; the Sequence is not a process: "Be" acting, instantly removes the hub of the wheel of fortune.

XCIX

As Presence becomes more permanent it refines the physical body.

C

Our Sequence is still like young Pinocchio, and we are trying to show him the way to school for the first time, but the nine of clubs tries to lure him with its tricks, so it is imperative to find all its tricks uninteresting. Also, it is important to observe what subject essence finds always interesting, and pay especial attention when they emerge. The nine of clubs knows essence is always easy to tempt, since its mechanical likes and dislikes remain the same for life and are natural and legitimate. So the steward must not become permissive, and firmly ban subjects of imagination and activities that lure us into a state of essence in sleep.

Don't let Pinocchio fall in the hands of the cat and the fox.

CI

The Sequence is not a mechanical effort, as it is uttered from a level of attention which per se requires a conscious effort. Besides, as soon as we say "Be", all dreams and nightmares arise against these six simple syllables; trying to disable and dissolve them into yet more dreams. How can such a struggle ever become mechanical?

Well, if it ever becomes mechanical, something else will have to be devised.

Suggested Readings

For a better understanding of the text:

By Peter Ouspensky:

The Psychology of Man's Possible Evolution
The Fourth Way
Talks with a Devil
In Search of the Miraculous

By Georges Gurdjieff
Views from the Real World
Meetings with Remarkable Men
Life is real only then, when I am

By Rodney Collin
Theory of Celestial Influence
Theory of Conscious Harmony

By Robert Burton
Self Remembering

By Girard Haven
Creating a Soul
Dear Friend

www.ingramcontent.com/pod-product-compliance
Ingram Content Group UK Ltd.
Pitfield, Milton Keynes, MK11 3LW, UK
UKHW041903230426
12049UKWH00020B/174/J